END TIMES

Practical Heavenly Mindedness

13 STUDIES FOR INDIVIDUALS OR GROUPS

LifeGuide®
BIBLE STUDIES

R. PAUL STEVENS

IVP Connect

An imprint of InterVarsity Press
Downers Grove, Illinois

InterVarsity Press
P.O. Box 1400, Downers Grove, IL 60515-1426
ivpress.com
email@ivpress.com

InterVarsity Press® *is the book-publishing division of InterVarsity Christian Fellowship/USA*®*, a movement of students and faculty active on campus at hundreds of universities, colleges and schools of nursing in the United States of America, and a member movement of the International Fellowship of Evangelical Students. For information about local and regional activities, visit intervarsity.org.*

LifeGuide® *is a registered trademark of InterVarsity Christian Fellowship.*

All Scripture quotations, unless otherwise indicated, are taken from the Holy Bible, New International Version®. NIV®. *Copyright* ©*1973, 1978, 1984 by International Bible Society. Used by permission of Zondervan Publishing House. All rights reserved.*

Cover image: Paul Nicklen/National Geographic Image Collection

ISBN 978-0-8308-3072-5

Printed in the United States of America ∞

P	27	26	25	24	23	22	21	20	19	18
Y	29	28	27	26	25	24	23	22	21	20

Contents

Getting the Most Out of
End Times

Why study the subject of end times? Some of us have a fascination with numbers, dates, mysterious events and secret meanings to veiled prophecies. But for others "end times" brings up images of elaborate charts and misguided pronouncements by doomsday preachers whose predictions of the end keep passing unfulfilled.

The study of end times is a very personal subject. It addresses fundamental questions that every person asks: What will happen when I die? Will the world end with a fizzle or a bang? Will things get worse or better? Does my work in this world have any lasting significance? Why be good if the world will be blown up anyway? What will heaven be like? And who will go there?

These studies from both the Old and New Testaments will address these and other questions. All too often "authoritative" books on last things concentrate on one or two passages in the Bible. In contrast, the book of Revelation, for example, gathers up themes, images and concepts threaded throughout the Old Testament. We need to look to the whole of Scripture for information.

We start with Acts 2 because the outpouring of the Holy Spirit after the resurrection of Jesus signaled the beginning of the last days. Central to last things is the conviction that Jesus will return in glory to receive his own. The words of Jesus in John 14 assure us of this; but they also show us how the Holy Spirit, now at work in our hearts, and the community of Christ are a tangible pledge of the reunion to come. Then we turn to some of the words of Jesus in Mark 13 concerning the fall of Jerusalem (in his own day) and his own return in the future. Our study of 2 Thessalonians 2 helps us understand the reality that believers encounter radical evil in this world as they attempt to live and work for God, evil that will become focused in a single individual before the end comes. Joel 2 is the prophecy referred to by Peter in his Pentecost sermon; but this study will shows us that the Day of the Lord has already begun, though it's yet to be fulfilled. Our ultimate future personally is not merely the immortality of the soul but the resurrection of the body (1 Corinthians 15). But resurrection and the other events surrounding the Lord's Second Coming do not mean bypassing the last judgment, a subject we take up in the context of the prophet Malachi's words to Israel. Our study of the future of the church and the future of the earth takes us into Ezekiel's vision of a renewed earth. The last five studies focus on the practical implications: waiting hopefully (Matthew 25), living righteously (2 Peter), making forever friends (Luke 16), investing in heaven (1 and 2 Thessalonians) and getting ready for the Lamb's wedding (Revelation 7; 19; 21).

These studies may not satisfy the longing of some to have a fixed timetable of end-times events or a comprehensive chart that coordinates all the images and metaphors of Scripture. But the effect of some end-times schemes can be to take away the mystery of God's final work and attempt to manage it. Actually, everything we need to know to live in Christ is abundantly clear—now and forever.

Getting God's story right can have many positive fruits. For example, it will help us view time as a gift to be received rather than a resource to be managed. It will show us that work done in this world may, in some way beyond our imagination, contribute to a world without end. We will be inspired to holy living since we are preparing ourselves for a great rendezvous with the Lord himself. We will be motivated to share the good news of Jesus since the delay in his coming is simply to give people maximum opportunity to turn to God, and to give his children maximum opportunity to share what they know. Responsible stewardship of the earth will become a priority as our future is not to be in a "spiritual" heaven but in a new heaven and a new earth. Daily work will be seen as a meaningful contribution to the kingdom of God that will outlast this world. It will liberate us from our need to save the world to see that the future is ultimately in God's hands and he will bring his kingdom to consummation his own way at his own time. Finally, it will equip us to live practically in this world with a healthy desire for heaven. C. S. Lewis is quoted as saying that if we find that nothing in this world *ultimately* satisfies us, it is a powerful argument that we were made for a better world and a better life.

It is mystery that saves me. But mystery in earnest, not just a puzzle. Mystery is God's inscrutable way of doing business. Mystery as the way he steers the bicycle of history with his hands in his pockets. Nothing is shoved, nothing is jimmied; nothing need ever be anything but true to itself. He never even touches the handlebars!*

Suggestions for Individual Study

1. As you begin each study, pray that God will speak to you through his Word.

2. Read the introduction to the study and respond to the personal reflection question or exercise. This is designed to help you focus on God and on the theme of the study.

3. Each study deals with a particular passage—so that you can delve into the author's meaning in that context. Read and reread the passage to be studied. The questions are written using the language of the New International Version, so you may wish to use that version of the Bible. The New Revised Standard Version is also recommended.

4. This is an inductive Bible study, designed to help you discover for yourself what Scripture is saying. The study includes three types of questions. *Observation* questions ask about the basic facts: who, what, when, where and how. *Interpretation* questions delve into the meaning of the passage. *Application* questions help you discover the implications of the text for growing in Christ. These three keys unlock the treasures of Scripture.

Write your answers to the questions in the spaces provided or in a personal journal. Writing can bring clarity and deeper understanding of yourself and of God's Word.

5. It might be good to have a Bible dictionary handy. Use it to look up any unfamiliar words, names or places.

6. Use the prayer suggestion to guide you in thanking God for what you have learned and to pray about the applications that have come to mind.

7. You may want to go on to the suggestion under "Now or Later," or you may want to use that idea for your next study.

---

*Robert Farrar Capon, *An Offering of Uncles: The Priesthood of Adam and the Shape of the World* (New York: Crossroad, 1982), p. 50.

Suggestions for Members of a Group Study

1. Come to the study prepared. Follow the suggestions for individual study mentioned above. You will find that careful preparation will greatly enrich your time spent in group discussion.

2. Be willing to participate in the discussion. The leader of your group will not be lecturing. Instead, he or she will be encouraging the members of the group to discuss what they have learned. The leader will be asking the questions that are found in this guide.

3. Stick to the topic being discussed. Your answers should be based on the verses which are the focus of the discussion and not on outside authorities such as commentaries or speakers. These studies focus on a particular passage of Scripture. Only rarely should you refer to other portions of the Bible. This allows for everyone to participate in in-depth study on equal ground.

4. Be sensitive to the other members of the group. Listen attentively when they describe what they have learned. You may be surprised by their insights! Each question assumes a variety of answers. Many questions do not have "right" answers, particularly questions that aim at meaning or application. Instead the questions push us to explore the passage more thoroughly.

When possible, link what you say to the comments of others. Also, be affirming whenever you can. This will encourage some of the more hesitant members of the group to participate.

5. Be careful not to dominate the discussion. We are sometimes so eager to express our thoughts that we leave too little opportunity for others to respond. By all means participate! But allow others to also.

6. Expect God to teach you through the passage being discussed and through the other members of the group. Pray that you will have an enjoyable and profitable time together, but also that as a result of the study you will find ways that you can take action individually and/or as a group.

7. Remember that anything said in the group is considered confidential and should not be discussed outside the group unless specific permission is given to do so.

8. If you are the group leader, you will find additional suggestions at the back of the guide.

1

The Last Days Are Here!

Acts 2

Like small children on a long journey, when we think about end times, we keep asking, "Are we almost there?"

GROUP DISCUSSION. What world events and life experiences have contributed to your view of the future of the human race and the future of planet earth? Are you optimistic or pessimistic? Why?

PERSONAL REFLECTION. What do you think and how do you feel when someone says, "The end of the world is near"?

According to the apostles of Jesus, the last days began with the ascension of Jesus to heaven and the outpouring of the Spirit on the church. And we have been in the last days ever since—almost two thousand years of last days! Indeed, the last days will continue until Christ comes again. It is hard to keep a balanced perspective on this. This study shows that in one sense we have "arrived," but in another sense we are still waiting. To keep the balance we must learn how to live "to the hilt" in these days of fulfillment while waiting hopefully for the last of the last days. *Read Acts 2:1-41.*

1. Jesus has been crucified and resurrected. He has also ascended into heaven out of sight (1:9). What happens to the waiting disciples to assure them that Jesus will continue to expand his worldwide mission?

2. The Feast of Pentecost (fifty days after the Passover) was one of the three great festivals of Israel. Why do you think Luke, the author, is careful to note the countries of origin represented by the visitors to Jerusalem for this great feast (vv. 9-11)?

3. When, if ever, have you experienced deep fellowship with people from other races and cultures whom you would normally have difficulty communicating with?

4. With what arguments does Peter counter the charge that he and his friends were intoxicated (v. 13)?

5. Peter explains the strange events of this feast day in terms of the Old Testament prophecy of Joel (Joel 2:28-31). What evidence does Peter give that he is correct in claiming the "day of the Lord" (v. 20, the last days) has arrived? (Note that he quotes Psalm 16:8-11 and Psalm 110:1, which are generally regarded as pointing to the Messiah.)

6. The "day of the LORD" (the last days) in Joel 2:1 is a day of both searing judgment on evildoers and gracious salvation and fulfillment for true servants of God (Joel 2:28-31). Interpreting this passage, Peter does not pronounce irrevocable doom on unbelievers and the executioners of Jesus, but rather stresses the grace of the day of the Lord. Why do you think he does this?

What hope does this bring for people today who are currently rejecting Jesus as their Lord and Savior?

_____

7. What must people do to respond to the arrival of the last days (v. 38)?

_____

8. What evidence in the text suggests that the Spirit outpoured on Pentecost is now the permanent endowment of the church for its mission in the world?

What indication is there that Pentecost might be a one-time event?

_____

9. In very few places of the world today are people asking Christians, "What shall we do?" (v. 37). Why do you think this is so?

10. *Read Acts 2:42-47.* What clues do we have in the passage to explain the growth of the church (v. 47) then and today?

---

11. What does living "in the last days" now mean to you?

Ask the Holy Spirit to continue to fill the church with love, joy and empowered mission.

Now or Later

Years after the first Pentecost the apostle Paul was racing across the Mediterranean to present a love gift from the Gentile churches to the relatively poor Jewish believers in Palestine. He was determined to do this in the annual feast of Pentecost. *Read Acts 20:16; 21:4-14; Romans 15:23-29; 2 Corinthians 8-9.* Why do you think presenting this gift at Pentecost might be important for Paul and for the wider church? In what ways would this ministry of giving constitute an authentic extension of the Spirit's outpouring on Pentecost? Community of language leads to community of property (Acts 2:42-47). Some dimensions of the community life of the first Christians reflect the emergency situation of pilgrims stranded in Jerusalem after the feast or not wanting to go home and leave this new community. What, however, are the dimensions of living in the last days that can be applied to your own life in this present age?

A Christian is a controlled drunk,
purposively intoxicated with the joy of the life
which is perpetually created by God himself.
CANON EVANS

2

He Will Come Back

The word *heaven* brings various images to people's minds. An old Christian song says, "This world is not my home. I'm just-a passing through. My treasures are laid up, somewhere beyond the blue."

GROUP DISCUSSION. What thoughts and feelings do the words of this song evoke?

PERSONAL REFLECTION. In Robert Frost's poem "Death of a Hired Hand," the hired hand Silas comes home to die. The old farmer, reflecting on the inconvenience this will mean, says, "Home is the place where, when you have to go there, they have to take you in." The farmer's wife had a better grasp of the matter when she replied, "I should have called it something you somehow haven't to deserve."* What thoughts and feelings does the word *home* awaken in you?

In this study we discover how Jesus in his farewell address promises an eternal home to his followers. Remarkably, in John's Gospel the time between the farewell of Jesus in his earthly body until his Second

Coming is not a time of empty waiting. If we will one day have an eternal *dwelling* with God, we may immediately have a real experience of the presence of Jesus through the *indwelling* of the Holy Spirit, called the Comforter or Advocate in John's Gospel. John's special contribution to end-times living is his emphasis on the continuity between life in Christ now (through the Spirit) and the life we will have when the end fully comes. In both cases our home with God is "something you somehow haven't to deserve"—a matter of sheer grace. *Read John 14:1-14.*

1. What indications does Jesus give that our ultimate destiny is much more than a mere place like an unassigned hotel room (vv. 1-4)?

2. What reason does Jesus give here for the importance of his coming back a second time after his death and resurrection?

3. How is it possible for true disciples of Jesus *to decide* not to be troubled as they face the unknown future, even the prospect of death?

4. How does this promise of Jesus help you to face your life-challenges with faith rather than fear?

5. What deep need does Jesus claim to meet through his answer to Thomas's question (vv. 5-7)?

6. What ultimate desire does Jesus claim to satisfy through his answer to Philip's question (vv. 8-10)?

7. *Read John 14:15-27.* What fresh meaning does Jesus now bring to the statement "I will come to you" (14:18)?

8. What new dimension of the meaning of "home" does Jesus now explore (v. 23)?

9. In what ways will the presence of the Counselor, the Holy Spirit, be an appearance of Christ?

Why will the coming of the Spirit *not* be the complete Second Coming of Jesus?

10. How does your present experience of the Spirit affect your time of waiting for Jesus to come back?

11. What prerequisites must be met to be "at home" with God?

Thank the Father, Son and Spirit for making a home in you.

Now or Later

The passage as a whole provides multiple reasons for believing in Jesus: (1) To believe in Jesus is the same as to believe in God (v. 1), that is, faith in Jesus is not something additional to believing in God since there is no other way to God than through Jesus (v. 6). (2) The words of Jesus are not his own but are the true words of God (v. 6). (3) The works that Jesus does are signs that point to God who is working through him. The "greater works" that will be accomplished by disciples when Jesus leaves are most probably centered in the mighty works of conversion that will be accomplished through the Spirit.

> *The coming of the Holy Ghost was not merely to*
> *supply the absence of the Son but to complete His presence.*
> BISHOP GORE

---

*Robert Frost, "Death of a Hired Hand," in *The Poems of Robert Frost* (New York: Random House, 1946), pp. 41-42.

3

Signs of the Times

Mark 13

Occasionally a dying parent or a dear friend has the privilege of saying goodbye and sharing their final words with those they love. Such words are so pregnant with meaning that one hangs on the meaning of every phrase.

GROUP DISCUSSION. When, if ever, have you heard a person's final words in this life? What was that like?

PERSONAL REFLECTION. What subjects would be uppermost in your own mind if you were given one last chance to speak with those you love?

This study covers Jesus' final words of warning and encouragement to his disciples about two coming events: one that would happen in the lifetime of the first disciples and another that may take place in ours. While the chapter is considered one of the most difficult in the Gospel of Mark, it contains an encouraging promise. Since God brought about the events that Jesus prophesied would take place in the lifetime of the first disciples, he will certainly accomplish the final event. In this study we will explore the connection between the two and learn how to be watchful. *Read Mark 13.*

1. Overlooking the temple from the Mount of Olives, Jesus and the disciples would have an excellent view of Herod's temple, described as a mountain of white marble covered with pure gold. What terrible events does Jesus predict (vv. 1-13)?

What disappointments does Jesus prepare the disciples to face?

2. In what ways have disasters and false spiritualities today suggested to you that the end may have come?

3. Jesus says (of the destruction of the temple) that these things will happen "in this generation" (v. 30). In what ways will the Second Coming of Jesus (the Son of Man) more than compensate for the loss of the temple?

4. In your own words, what answer does Jesus give to the disciples' questions in verse 4: "When will these things happen?" and "what will be the sign that they are about to be fulfilled?"

5. Jesus describes the necessity of being ready for an escape to a safe haven. What might divert disciples from watching carefully for the signs of these times and from readiness for their escape (vv. 5-23)?

6. How does Jesus' language express the absolute dominion with which he will reign as King when he comes (vv. 26-27)?

---

7. Why is it significant that the elect are gathered "from the four winds, from the ends of the earth to the ends of the heavens" (v. 27)?

What is the relationship of this prophecy of a great gathering to the first prophecy of the destruction of the *physical* temple?

---

8. Which character do you identify with in verses 32-37?

---

9. The Second Coming of Jesus will mean for each individual what his or her death will mean: the end of one's personal world. What will it mean for you to live each day with your bags packed up and ready to go?

---

10. How will you "be on your guard" for diversions and "keep watch" for the coming of the Son of Man both in times of social disruption and in times of relative security?

Ask the Lord to help you to be watchful of the time, to be ready for his coming and to be fruitfully occupied until he comes again.

Now or Later

The Second Coming of Jesus is the most important promise about the future. Research the purposes of the Second Coming (1) for victory, as the final triumph of God's kingdom (1 Corinthians 15:24), (2) for judgment, as the ratifying of destinies (1 Corinthians 4:5), (3) for salvation, the final glory of the saints (Colossians 3:4; 1 Thessalonians 4:16), (4) for new creation both of mortal humans (1 Corinthians 15:50-55) and the decaying cosmos (Romans 8:21; 2 Peter 3:13; Revelation 21:1) and (5) for the glory of God (2 Thessalonians 1:10) (J. I. Packer, "Notes on Systematic Theology IV," Regent College, Vancouver, B.C.).

Apocalypse is arson—it secretly sets a fire in
the imagination that boils the fat out of an obese
culture-religion and renders a clear gospel love,
a pure gospel hope, a purged gospel faith.

EUGENE PETERSON

4

Grappling with Radical Evil

2 Thessalonians 2

In every generation following Jesus is hard. But in some generations it is especially hard when political, social, cultural and religious forces gang up against the beleaguered Christian church. Is God really in control of the world? This question, asked by ordinary people when they read the newspaper, strikes a deep chord in the human heart. Followers of Jesus are not immune to bad news.

GROUP DISCUSSION. Under what circumstances have you wondered whether God was still in charge?

PERSONAL REFLECTION. What pressures from society most frustrate your desire to live by the teachings of Jesus?

It is normal for believers to experience pressure, because they live in two worlds at once: the new age inaugurated by Jesus and the old age that persists until Jesus comes again. But in this study the apostle Paul envisions a day when the powers of evil will be "incarnated" in a widespread rebellion (an anti-kingdom) and personified in a single individual (an antichrist). As we will discover, this encounter with radical evil is the experience of every generation of Christians waiting for the end, but especially of the generation that precedes the glorious coming of Jesus again. Perhaps, as Bonhoeffer once said, when there is not an inch of space on earth left where it is safe to be a Christian, the Lord will come. The bad news precedes the best news of all. *Read 2 Thessalonians 2.*

1. What alarming situation in the church in Thessalonica prompts Paul to address the subject of end times (vv. 1-2)?

2. In what ways will the coming of the "man of lawlessness" affect the life and witness of Christians (vv. 3-4)?

3. What evidence do we have of the beginnings of these evil times in our own day and culture?

4. Suppose the Thessalonians believed the false teaching that the Lord had already come. What would the prospect of encountering the man of lawlessness then mean to them, or to us?

5. In what ways does Paul account for the fact that the full mystery of evil is not yet apparent in the world (vv. 5-8)?

6. What are the characteristics of this evil regime that make responding appropriately, even for Christians, not a simple, clear-cut matter (vv. 8-12)?

7. What can the Thessalonian believers do to become equipped to stand firm in the face of present and future threats (vv. 13-15)?

8. What is God prepared to do to equip Christians to stand firm?

9. Taking this passage as a whole, why should believers not be taken by surprise at the Second Coming of Jesus?

10. Where is God at work in the ambiguous situation described in the passage?

Where is God at work in the ambiguous situations of your life?

Ask God to teach you how to live faithfully, with integrity and discernment in all the ambiguities of your own life situation.

Now or Later

Compare the "man of lawlessness" prophecy in 2 Thessalonians with the two beasts in Revelation 13. They attempt to control the whole world (the beast from the sea, 13:1-10) and to use religion and spirituality (the beast from the earth, 13:11-18) to enforce the political authority of the first beast. In the first century this was an obvious reference to the Roman emperor and emperor worship. But what indications are there that all of this prophecy was not fulfilled in the first century and will find its consummation in a total evil person and regime? See also Revelation 14:11 where the two beasts are referred to simply as "the beast."

> *History is not a random series of meaningless events.*
> *It is rather a succession of periods and happenings*
> *which are under the sovereign rule of God,*
> *who is the God of history.*
> JOHN STOTT

5

God's Timing—
and Ours

Joel 2:12-32

"I never have enough time!" "We are having the time of our lives." "I knew my time had come."

We experience time in many different ways. Old Testament prophets understood that God would intervene in the normal sequence of historical events with his own kind of time (*kairos*), time infused with judgment and grace. This is transparent time in which we see through what is happening and view events from God's perspective. The effect when clock time becomes significant time is something like the moment when, in the middle of a boring lecture (clock time), a professor announces a surprise test that will determine whether the student will pass or fail (significant, eternal time). Clock time is a resource that can be managed; God's time is a gift to be received.

GROUP DISCUSSION. Recall an experience of "losing track of (clock) time" because you were caught up in a totally engaging activity.

PERSONAL REFLECTION. When in your experience has ordinary clock time (that goes on and on) seemingly "stood still" because something vitally important was happening?

The move from clock time to eternal time is part of the meaning of the Old Testament concept of the day of the Lord. In Joel 2:1-11 the prophet was writing more than four centuries before Christ. He explained that the plague of locusts swarming over Judah and destroying the land was a definite judgment of God on the disobedience of his own people. This was their first experience of the day of the Lord (2:1, 11), a day which did not exempt God's own people from judgment. By studying the prophecy of Joel, we will deepen our grasp not only of how Jesus inaugurated the end times but also of how much more we should anticipate the full realization of the day of the Lord. *Read Joel 2:12-32.*

1. On what characteristics of God does Joel base his promise that God will alter his present course of total judgment (vv. 12-17)?

2. *National* repentance was appropriate for a nation-church like Israel under the old covenant. In what ways should the Lord's people today express their repentance now that the church and the state cannot be completely identified?

3. Imagine what it would be like to see a whole congregation repent. What sins of a people or a nation would require such a dramatic change of direction?

4. What material blessings wait for the Lord's people if they repent (vv. 18-27)?

5. Verses 28-32 further elaborate the results of repentance on the day of the Lord. What supernatural benefits will come to Israel "afterward"?

6. How are these spiritual gifts, signs and securities indications of a deeper fulfillment of Israel's covenant relationship with God?

7. In what ways does Joel's prophecy of an Old Testament "Pentecost" go beyond the normal experience of the people of God before Christ?

8. In quoting Joel on the day of Pentecost (Acts 2:16-21), Peter made an important change. Instead of saying "afterward" (Joel 2:28), he inserted a phrase from another prophecy about the day of the Lord in Isaiah 2:2—"in the last days" (Acts 2:17). Why is this change of time important in light of the events of Pentecost?

9. In Joel's prophecy, repentance followed by forgiveness would inaugurate the day of the Lord and bring about an age of Messianic blessing. Peter reversed the order, calling for repentance *because* of the events of that day. Why are repentance and calling on the name of the Lord (Joel 2:32; Acts 2:21) so essential at the time of God's intervention?

What does this interpretation of the flexible *order* in which things will happen (while retaining the essential truths) suggest about the relation of end-time events to our kind of clock and calendar time?

10. The elaborate imagery of cosmic, irreversible changes common in Old Testament prophecy and used by Joel (vv. 30-31; Acts 2:19-20) shows that in the day of the Lord nothing will ever be the same again. How can that be true for you today?

---

11. What answer can you give to the person who wonders whether God will restore in their life "the years the locusts have eaten" (v. 25)?

Ask Jesus to come.

Now or Later

Like distant mountain peaks that appear to be merged without revealing the depth of the hidden valleys between, Joel pictures multiple realities without assigning their place on a timeline or showing how deep the valleys are between the peaks. In the New Testament there are six "peaks" of God-revelation at the end, again without our knowing the exact order. Examine how each of them contributes to the full meaning of the end: the Second Coming of Jesus (Acts 1:10-11; 1 Thessalonians 5:2-3; 2 Thessalonians 1:7-9); the resurrection of the body (1 Corinthians 15:12-58); the last judgment (John 5:22; Acts 17:30-31; 2 Corinthians 5:10); eternal life (John 6:47; Romans 6:23); the full coming of the kingdom of God (Luke 13:29; 1 Corinthians 15:24); the new heaven and new earth (Revelation 21—22).

> *Like so many Old Testament promises,*
> *this passage bursts its original wrappings and leaps into*
> *the New Testament with wider and deeper significance.*
> LESLIE ALLEN

6

The Future of the Human Person

1 Corinthians 15:12-28, 35-44, 58

A man once asked a church warden what he thought would happen to him when he died. "I shall immediately depart into eternal happiness," he replied, then added, "but I wish you would not talk to me about such an unpleasant subject!"

GROUP DISCUSSION. What evidence do you see in culture of how we deny death by pampering and prolonging the life of our mortal bodies? Where have you heard the perspective that the body is evil and is a hindrance?

PERSONAL REFLECTION. The ancient Greeks had a low view of bodily life and regarded salvation as liberation from the body. The Bible offers a high view of the body as created by God for his glory. Which view was uppermost in your own upbringing? Explain.

Almost no one wants to die! However, unless we are present on earth when Christ comes again, death is one step toward our final existence in Christ. That final existence involves being fully human persons, equipped with a spiritual body to be with Jesus and his people in a perfect environment. That ultimate hope of our own resurrection, founded on the fact of Christ's resurrection, makes a difference in how we live our bodily life now. *Read 1 Corinthians 15:12-28.*

1. Apparently some Christians in Corinth had stopped believing (or had never believed) in their own future bodily resurrection. What does Paul say are the consequences of this belief (vv. 12-15)?

2. Paul is arguing from something accepted by the Corinthians—that Christ *was* raised from the dead. What will be the consequences if this fundamental fact is denied (vv. 16-19)?

3. What difference does Christ's resurrection make to the way we approach our own inevitable death?

4. In what ways does verse 19 run counter to the contemporary Western view of Christian living?

5. Why would being a new creature in Christ *only in this life* not be enough?

6. What does the resurrection of Christ ("the firstfruits," v. 20) guarantee for the rest of us?

7. The Greeks viewed death as a release for the soul. Why does Paul take a less positive view (vv. 21-26)?

8. *Read 1 Corinthians 15:35-44.* Paul turns now to the question of what form the future existence of believers will take. What similarities and differences will exist between this life and the next?

9. What new ideas about heaven have you gained from this study thus far?

10. *Read 1 Corinthians 15:58.* How does Paul's final exhortation encourage you today?

11. Taken as a whole, how does this study show that our own future resurrection brings great meaning to our life and work as Christians now?

Present your body to Christ as a living sacrifice and with it all your bodily life—work, sleep, eating, walking, touching and making things.

Now or Later

Elsewhere (1 Corinthians 6:12-20; 15:32-34) Paul insists that resurrection hope calls for the repudiation of sexual immorality and an "immediate gratification" approach to life. Read these passages. Consider how the biblical view of the body could change sexual behavior and the pressure today to "have it all now."

> *As little as babies in their mothers' bodies know about their arrival, just so little do we know about eternal life.*
> MARTIN LUTHER

7

The Beautiful Judgment of God

Judgment. Hardly what most people look forward to, whether from a parent, a church leader, an employer or a court of law.

GROUP DISCUSSION. Do you see judgment as a positive or negative function?

PERSONAL REFLECTION. Describe an experience of judgment in your family upbringing. What was hopeful in that experience, or what left you feeling hopeless?

Hardly anyone, if given the opportunity, would choose to face the judgment of God at the end of time. But contrary to our normal way of envisioning the future, many Old Testament saints longed for the judgment of God because they lived in a society in which justice was often denied to the ordinary person. Malachi, a relatively unknown prophet, was convicted that God would hold his covenant people accountable for what they knew and how they lived. Malachi's perspective makes an important contribution to understanding how to live in the end times. He paints a picture of a judgment that also offers hope. *Read Malachi 2:17—3:5.*

1. What response does the prophet make to those who say things like "God appears to favor the wicked" and "life is not fair"?

2. When, in your life, have you said or thought this?

How do you react to Malachi's response?

3. The identity of the "messenger of the covenant" is shrouded in mystery. What effect will the coming of this person have on the people of God waiting for the Lord's coming (3:2-3)?

4. Find the images Malachi uses to describe the judgment of God (3:2-3). From these images what do we learn about the Lord's purpose in judging his own covenant people?

5. In the light of this, why do you think judgment begins at the sanctuary and with the priestly tribe of Levites (see 1 Peter 4:17)?

6. In contrast to the refining process in 3:2-4, what will God's judgment mean to those in the community who persist in disobedient living (3:5)?

7. Why do you think the Bible connects true holiness with concern for social righteousness?

8. In what ways has Malachi answered those who ask, "Where is the God of justice" (2:17)?

9. *Read Malachi 3:13—4:3.* What assurance does Malachi give to those who feel that living righteously "does not pay" (3:17-18)?

10. Assuming that the people mentioned in 3:14 are the same as those "who feared the LORD" (3:16), what do we learn about living in the light of God's judgment?

11. How is the judgment here different from that which is applied to God's own people (4:1-3)?

12. God's people, while exempt from final condemnation, are not free from evaluation. What difference will this make to the way you live?

Thank God that you are not left to invent the meaning of your own life. Ask that in the end you may be found in him and all that you have done in this life be refined in fire and, purged of sin, find its place in the new heaven and new earth.

Now or Later

The final passage of the book—not included in this study—takes up again the messenger of 3:1 as the precursor of "that great and dreadful day of the LORD" (4:5). *Read Malachi 3:1—4:6.* This time, however, Elijah is named as the messenger who will prepare the way. Jesus considered John the Baptist as both the messenger (Malachi 3:1; Matthew 11:10) and Elijah (Malachi 4:5; Matthew 11:14), though John rejected the notion that he fulfilled the Elijah prophecy (John 1:21). John the Baptist was profoundly influenced by the prophecy of Malachi, to the extent that his hope for a fiery judgment was undoubtedly not fulfilled in the ministry of Jesus (Matthew 3:11-12; Luke 3:16-17) Joyce Baldwin brilliantly explains how this Old Testament prophecy of final judgment was ultimately fulfilled in the New Testament: "An interval separated the first and second comings and the day of grace was extended to delay final judgment. This does not mean, however, that judgment has been averted. The warning that ends the Old Testament is not absent at the end of the New (Revelation 22:10-15), but the difference is that there grace has the last word (verse 21)" (Joyce C. Baldwin, *Haggai, Zechariah, Malach: An Introduction and Commentary* [Downers Grove: InterVarsity Press, 1972), p. 253).

The most stupendous thought of which the mind is capable is that of personal accountability to Almighty God.

DANIEL WEBSTER

8

Imagining the
New Heaven and the
New Earth

Ezekiel 43:1-12; 47:1-12

Paul Marshall titled one of his books *Heaven Is Not My Home*. Our future in Christ is not to be a saved soul in heaven but to be a fully resurrected person in a new heaven and new earth. We do not "go" to heaven! According to the last book of the Bible, heaven comes to earth.

GROUP DISCUSSION. Why do you think "the new earth" is so often dropped from our consideration of eternal life?

PERSONAL REFLECTION. To a large extent imagination has been quenched in contemporary Western culture. In what ways, however, do you find your own imagination stimulated?

In reality, heaven is no mere "pie in the sky by and by" but our true homeland: a total life in a total environment with the presence of God as the center and source of everything. The Old Testament prophet

Ezekiel was given the vision of the ultimate Jewish homeland while he was in exile in Babylon. Ezekiel's vision of the temple, the new Jerusalem and the Israelites resettled in the redesigned land of Israel was the ultimate Old Testament hope. Drawing heavily on the imagery of Ezekiel and Isaiah (65:17-25), John envisions for Christians in Revelation 21—22 an even greater hope: a completely renewed creation. Jesus says, "I am making everything new" (Revelation 21:5), words which Ezekiel would have welcomed with all his heart. We should too. *Read Ezekiel 43:1-12.*

---

1. Nineteen years earlier (10:18-22; 11:22-24) Ezekiel had seen the glory of the Lord leaving the temple. Now he has a second encounter with God like that at the Kebar River in Babylon. What sights, sounds, words and movements contribute to Ezekiel's sense of over-powering awe?

---

2. When, if ever, have you been moved to worship by sights, sounds, words or movements?

---

3. What encouraging word does God give to Ezekiel (vv. 6-12)?

---

4. For what purpose should Ezekiel pass this on to the people (vv. 10-12)?

---

5. What needs among the Israelites in exile would be met by the

Lord's summary statement "This is where I will live among the Israelites forever" (v. 7)?

---

6. The law of the temple (v. 12) is the principle of holiness. What will dwelling with God require of those who hunger for God's presence?

---

7. The last book of the Bible (Revelation 21—22) draws heavily from the imagery of the new Jerusalem pictured in Ezekiel 40—48, but *without* the temple. Why would a future *with* a temple be essential for an Israelite "heaven," but *without* one be even more appropriate for followers of Jesus who want to dwell with him forever (Revelation 21:22)?

---

8. In Revelation 22:1-3 John uses Ezekiel's vision to express the consummation of Christ's full and final presence and purpose. *Read Ezekiel 47:1-12.* What significant truths are communicated by this exquisite vision?

---

9. Why are such imaginative visions of heaven more helpful to our faith than detailed blueprints?

---

10. What difference should this vision of a renewed creation (and not merely a renewed worship center) make to our stewardship of the created world?

11. It has been said that no worse fate can befall a person than to be completely at home in this life. Do you agree? Why or why not?

12. What new perspectives on eternal life have you gained from this study?

Ask God to open the eyes of your heart to see the height and depth of his greatness and the love of Jesus which passes all understanding.

Now or Later

Read Revelation 21—22. John uses and expands on Ezekiel's vision of our final destiny as a presence (of God), people and a place. Read also Isaiah 65:17-25 on which John draws as he proclaims that Jesus will make everything new (Revelation 21:5). In what way does the enlarged picture of Christ's saving work deepen your reverence for Christ and your practical discipleship?

> *The Christians who did most for the present world*
> *were just those who thought most about the next. . . .*
> *It is since Christians have largely ceased to think of the other world*
> *that they have become so ineffective in this.*
> *Aim at heaven and you will get earth "thrown in":*
> *aim at earth and you will get neither.*
> C. S. LEWIS

9

Waiting with Hope

Matthew 25:1-13, 31-46

Waiting is not easy, especially if the future is uncertain or threatening. In reaction to fear about the future we may develop a short-range attitude that embraces an instant-gratification culture. They squeeze every pleasure they can out of the moment because there may not be another one. Even Christians are profoundly influenced by short-term future thinking and, forgetting the glorious prospect of fulfillment in the new heaven and the new earth, try to get "the best of both worlds" by pulling everything they can out of this life while they wait—without any real hope—for the next. Other Christians respond by interpreting the prayer "Come, Lord Jesus" (Revelation 22:20) as a prayer for instant evacuation.

GROUP DISCUSSION. What evidence do you see of fear about the future in contemporary culture, literature, music or drama?

PERSONAL REFLECTION. How do you react when a person you are waiting for is delayed? Why do you think you react the way you do?

Two parables of Jesus—the ten virgins, and the sheep and the goats—provide two crucial dimensions of the spirituality of waiting. *Read Matthew 25:1-13.*

1. "At that time" refers to the day of the coming of the Lord (Matthew 24:42). In what ways was the behavior of the wise and foolish virgins similar as they waited for the coming of the groom?

How were their behaviors different?

2. Both the foolish and the wise *wanted* a short wait. What evidence do we have that the wise were also ready for a long wait?

3. What difference will it make to your lifestyle to be ready for a long wait while simultaneously being ready for the Lord to come immediately?

4. What do the terrible words of Jesus—"I don't know you" (v. 12)— tell us about the basis of final judgment?

5. *Read Matthew 25:31-46.* While another kingdom parable, this one adds the further note of final judgment. Who is present for the judgment?

6. On what basis are the sheep and the goats separated?

What is the ultimate end of each?

7. What does the surprise of the righteous (v. 39) indicate about the possible motives for the good works they did?

8. What does the defense of the unrighteous (v. 44) indicate about the deficiency of their faith?

9. What practical steps can you take to be ready, like the righteous, for the coming of the Son of Man?

10. In the light of the two parables, how can you wait for the end of the end times wisely and constructively?

Ask God to fill your heart with love for the least, the last and the lost.

Now or Later

Genuine righteousness involves more than consciously doing acts of charity with a view to gaining a reward from Jesus, or even pretending that the unpleasant poor person is the Lord Jesus, albeit masked. True love is guileless even in terms of religious benefit. Study another example of righteousness in the Old Testament—Job. Satan inferred that Job had ulterior motives for being right with God ("Does Job fear God for nothing?" [Job 1:9]). Then followed the excruciating test—the loss of everything. When, later, Job cries out, "Though he slay me, yet will I hope in him" (13:15), we have proof that Satan was wrong. Consider some of the New Testament passages that show that righteousness is not a contract in which we believe in God because things will go better with God or because of our performance: Romans 4:3, 9; Galatians 2:21; Philippians 3:9; Hebrews 11:7.

Happy are those whom [the judgment] finds laboring in their vocations,
whether they were merely going out to feed the pigs
or laying good plans to deliver humanity a hundred years hence
from some great evil. The curtain has indeed now fallen.
Those pigs will never in fact be fed, the great campaign against white
slavery or governmental tyranny will never in fact proceed to victory.
No matter, you were at your post when the inspection came.

C. S. LEWIS

10

Speeding the End

2 Peter 3

The prospect of the end of the world produces a variety of responses: denial, despair, passivity or frenetic activity. Influenced by the pessimism of secular society, couples are not sure they should conceive children and bring them into this kind of world, or whether they should keep the children they have conceived. They worry about the influence of drugs, AIDS and violence on the ones they love. People worry whether there will be jobs upon graduation and whether their marriages—if they marry at all—will last. It is hardly surprising that such world-weariness drives many young people to consider that the only thing worth doing in the world in these last days is to go into professional ministry.

GROUP DISCUSSION. Which reaction characterizes your own generation? people younger than you? older than you?

PERSONAL REFLECTION. What is your personal reaction to people who claim the world will probably end with either a fizzle or a big bang?

Followers of Jesus in the early church could not wait for the future to happen. They welcomed it, wanting not only to live in light of the end but to hasten the coming of the Lord Jesus. They believed that this event was such a positive finality that their whole view of the future could be shaped by that eschatological perspective. So Peter said, "You ought to live holy and godly lives as you look forward to the day of the Lord and speed its coming" (2 Peter 3:11-12). *Read 2 Peter 3:1-18.*

1. How does Peter respond to those who ridicule the hope of Christ's Second Coming?

2. A great deal of time has passed since the writing of this letter! How do you personally respond to the long delay?

3. On what grounds can we trust God's Word concerning not-yet-visible last things?

4. For what reason is God delaying the fulfillment of the promise (vv. 9-15)?

5. What are the implications of comparing Christ's coming to a thief's visit (v. 10)?

6. In what ways will Christ's Second Coming change everything (vv. 10-15)?

————————————————————————

7. Why is the Second Coming of Christ an incentive to holy living?

What effect should the Lord's coming have on your own lifestyle?

————————————————————————

8. Peter uses an enigmatic word in verse 12 which is sometimes translated "speed its coming." What indications are given in the passage that the Lord's restraint in bringing the story to a final conclusion is contingent on some of our actions?

————————————————————————

9. What help has Peter given to equip us to "grow in the grace and knowledge of our Lord and Savior Jesus Christ" (vv. 16-18)?

————————————————————————

10. What is your personal response to the challenge of speeding and eagerly waiting for the coming of Jesus?

Ask God to keep you from passively waiting for the end. Ask him to help you to do all you can to live the prayer "Thy kingdom come, Thy will be done, on earth as it is in heaven."

Now or Later

Eschatology is the most pastoral of all theological perspectives, showing how the future impinges on the present in such ways that the truth of the gospel is verified in life "in the middle." "It shows us that believers are not set 'at the high noon of life,' but at the dawn of a new day at the point where night and day, things passing and things to come, grapple with each other" (Jurgen Moltmann, *Theology of Hope*, trans. James W. Leitch [New York: Harper & Row, 1967], p. 31). Consider the difference between being a "morning person" and being an "afternoon person" as it relates to living and working hopefully.

> *The gospel is vastly more than an offer to men who care to*
> *accept it of a meaning for their personal lives.*
> *It is the declaration of God's cosmic purpose by which the*
> *whole public history of mankind is sustained and overruled,*
> *and by which men without exception will be judged. . . .*
> *It is the invitation to be fellow workers with God in the*
> *fulfillment of that purpose through the atoning work of Christ*
> *and through the witness of the Holy Spirit.*
> LESSLIE NEWBIGIN

11

Making Forever Friends

Luke 16

James M. Houston has said, "A true friend can never have a hidden motive for being a friend. He can have no hidden agenda. A friend is simply a friend, for the sake of friendship."*

GROUP DISCUSSION. Recall your most positive experience of friendship. What were some of the characteristics of the relationship?

PERSONAL REFLECTION. Recall an experience of being befriended by someone who had an ulterior motive. What was particularly disappointing about that experience?

"Use worldly wealth to gain friends for yourselves" (Luke 16:9) is a paradoxical command on the lips of Jesus. Friendship is not *for* anything, not even evangelism, and certainly not for personal advancement. But these enigmatic words of Jesus challenge us deeply to use our worldly resources with a view to building relationships that will last forever. Luke 16 has two "end times" events in view: the death of every one of us, and the death and resurrection of Jesus—which ought to be a convincing proof of his divinity. But neither event will mean what it should if we fail to use our resources in this life the way God intended. *Read Luke 16:1-18.*

1. In what ways could the owner find the manager's actions "commendable" (vv. 1-8)?

2. While not encouraging evil deceit, Jesus does commend shrewdness in his followers. In what ways might we exhibit a good form of shrewdness?

3. What evidence do we have in the text that Jesus is not merely thinking of everyday reversals of fortune but something more final (v. 9)?

4. What further instruction does Jesus give about being a steward or manager of the Lord's resources (vv. 10-18)? Why, then, is it impossible to be devoted to both God and money?

5. *Read Luke 16:19-31.* In what way can this be an example of *not* making friends through the use of one's material assets?

6. In the second parable, Jesus puts himself into the story as the poor man at the gate who, after he had died, contemplates the impact of coming back from the dead (vv. 27, 31). Earlier (vv. 16-18) Jesus related the matter of wealth to the Law and the Prophets, which address the need for justice and mercy expressed to the poor and powerless. Why do you think the resurrection of Jesus will not convince people who are presently disobeying the Law and Prophets on this issue?

7. The second parable (16:19-31) is a negative example of making friends through money. Give some positive examples.

8. What has your experience of making friends by means of money been like?

9. How would you now distinguish using money to make friends— self-interest disguised as altruism—and true friendship with the poor?

10. The poor can be "near" neighbors or "faraway" neighbors on the other side of the globe. How does serving the poor offer "true riches" (v. 11) that will survive death?

11. How do you need to change the way you use money?

Ask God to teach you to prize the treasure of relationships with holy shrewdness.

Now or Later

Consider some Old Testament examples of shrewdness: Rebekah's shrewd plan to get the right son blessed (Jacob) when her husband was determined to bless the wrong (but his favorite) son, Esau (Genesis 27:1-33); Jacob's scheme to provide a living for his own family from his stingy father-in-law (Genesis 30:25-43); Rahab the prostitute showing shrewdness in hiding the Hebrew spies (Joshua 2:1-16); Ehud's clever strategy to gain the advantage over Israel's enemy (Judges 3:12-30).

> *There was once a wild goose who went to live with some tame geese.*
> *He was committed to liberate them from their mediocre lives.*
> *The wild goose lived with the tame geese for a year,*
> *and he enjoyed the rich food, comfortable shelter and easy life.*
> *Each year, when the wild geese flew overhead,*
> *he would flutter his wings, prepare to join them*
> *but settle down again in the farmyard. Ten years passed and*
> *the wild goose became tame, and it forgot how to fly.*
> SØREN KIERKEGAARD

---

*James Houston, *Transforming Friendship* (Oxford, U.K.: Lion, 1989), pp. 195-96.

12

Investing in Heaven

1 Thessalonians 4:13—5:11; 2 Thessalonians 3:6-18

"Work for the night is coming," goes an old hymn. But as we have already seen, biblical eschatology tells us that we are on the verge of a new day.

GROUP DISCUSSION. What effect on your daily activities would these changed words have: "Work for the day is dawning"?

PERSONAL REFLECTION. What effect does a threatening catastrophe announced on the news have on your attitude toward your daily work?

In the Western world and much of Asia people are working themselves to death to become successful. The people Paul was writing to appeared to have the exact opposite problem. Writing in the Greek world, Paul was confronted by people inoculated against work by the culture. Work was seen as a curse, and to be out of work was a piece of singularly good fortune. Further, in his ministry in the Gentile churches, Paul had to face a problem that is still with us: when people become Christians they instinctively feel that the best way to serve God in gratitude would be to leave their "secular" jobs (and possibly their marriages) and "go into the ministry." This problem was exacerbated by the conviction held by many in the Thessalonian church that Jesus' coming was just around the corner. This text has a message both for those who are lazy and for those who are workholics. *Read 1 Thessalonians 4:13—5:11.*

1. What new perspectives does this passage bring regarding what will happen when Jesus comes back?

2. What will it mean for you to be "alert" and "self-controlled" (5:6)?

3. How does Paul comfort those whose loved ones died *before* the Lord's return (4:13-18; 5:10)?

4. What further information does Paul give us about the timing of the Lord's return (5:1-11)?

5. Why would this message be encouraging rather than threatening to Paul's friends in Thessalonica (4:18; 5:11)?

6. *Read 2 Thessalonians 3:6-18.* How does Paul answer the argument that if Jesus is coming back tomorrow there is no point in working today?

———————————————————————————

7. Why do you think Paul made such a strong example (3:9) and gave such strong teaching (3:14-15) on the relationship of work to end-times living?

———————————————————————————

8. In what ways are both idleness and workaholism symptoms of moral sloth and spiritual disease?

———————————————————————————

9. In light of this study how will you use your daily activities to invest in the Lord's coming and in heaven?

———————————————————————————

10. In light of all the studies, what new meaning does Paul's final blessing have: "The Lord be with all of you"?

Praise God our Creator, Sustainer, Redeemer and Consummator for the privilege of entering into his work.

Now or Later

Study some of the biblical teaching on work: God is a worker (Genesis 1:1, see also Robert Banks, *God the Worker*); work is a divine calling for human beings that includes making things, music, crafts, culture and meaning (Genesis 1:28; 2:15); work is frustrated by sin (Genesis 3:17-19; Ecclesiastes 2:17-23); work is a means of serving our neighbor (Ephesians 4:28); God receives our work (Colossians 3:22-24).

We can commit ourselves without reserve to all the secular work our shared humanity requires of us, knowing that nothing we do in itself is good enough to form part of that city's building, knowing that everything— from our most secret prayers to our most public political acts— is part of that sin-stained human nature that must go down into the valley of death and judgment, and yet knowing that as we offer it up to the Father in the name of Christ and in the power of the Spirit, it is safe with him and—purged in fire— it will find its place in the holy city at the end.

LESSLIE NEWBIGIN

13

Going to the Lamb's Wedding

George Bernard Shaw makes his character Don Juan say, "Heaven is all right, of course. But for meeting old friends and acquaintances, you can't beat hell." He thus shows a complete misunderstanding of the attractiveness of heaven. But he does reveal an insight which W. H. Auden takes up, namely, that no one is ever *sent* to hell; he or she insists on going there.

GROUP DISCUSSION. How do you react to the thought that no one is ever sent to hell (or heaven) that doesn't insist on going?

PERSONAL REFLECTION. What do you think living in heaven will be like?

God did not first of all think up creation and then consider where it all might end. He first of all thought about the marriage supper of the Lamb—that final rendezvous of Jesus with believers in a perfect environment (Revelation 19:7-9). And then God made a world to get ready for it. Our study in the last book of the Bible offers an empowering vision of our ultimate future—the party to come. In view of this, end-times living makes perfect sense. *Read Revelation 7:9-17.*

1. At the opening of each of the first six seals (chapter 6) cataclysmic events occur in the course of supercharged history. The seals symbolize that the events surrounding the Second Coming of Jesus are determined by God's sovereign purpose. Describe the appearance, position and words of the great multitude.

What evidence is there that this is the true church of Christ?

2. Imagine yourself as part of the multitude. What would you be thinking, saying, hearing and doing? Would you enjoy this?

3. On what basis do these believers stand in the presence of God?

4. How will their experience of Christ after death more than compensate for the trials they have experienced as they lived faithfully for Christ in this life?

5. Why would people unwilling to follow Christ find this an unappealing future environment?

6. *Read Revelation 19:1-10.* God has now finally dealt with the world system (Babylon) and its perverted culture (the harlot). What do the saints rejoice in?

---

7. The Lamb is an Old Testament image for the Messiah that came to be applied to Jesus because of its redemptive meaning. Why is the marriage of the Lamb a particularly appropriate metaphor for our future experience of the Second Coming of Christ?

---

8. On what basis could one be confident of being invited to the wedding?

---

9. *Read Revelation 21:1-9.* What new information do we gain about our final destiny in Christ?

---

10. How is this final vision much more than people commonly think of as "heaven"?

---

11. Knowing how the story ends, how can you shape your daily life now with a view to this wonderful future?

Pray "Come, Lord Jesus," and live in the light of heaven's triumphant cry: "The kingdom of the world has become the kingdom of our Lord and of his Christ, / and he will reign for ever and ever" (Revelation 11:15).

Now or Later

Consider the realities of the church as John writes to the seven churches in ancient Asia (Revelation 2—3). Then research the promises Jesus makes to them (2:7, 11, 17, 28; 3:5, 12, 21). Finally, investigate the final destiny of the people of God (Revelation 19; 21—22). Knowing this is the future of the church, what difference will this make to your present relationship to the people of God?

The only ultimate disaster that can befall us,
I have come to realize, is to feel ourselves to be at home here on earth.
MALCOLM MUGGERIDGE

Leader's Notes

MY GRACE IS SUFFICIENT FOR YOU. (2 COR 12:9)

Leading a Bible discussion can be an enjoyable and rewarding experience. But it can also be *scary*—especially if you've never done it before. If this is your feeling, you're in good company. When God asked Moses to lead the Israelites out of Egypt, he replied, "O LORD, please send someone else to do it!" (Ex 4:13). It was the same with Solomon, Jeremiah and Timothy, but God helped these people in spite of their weaknesses, and he will help you as well.

You don't need to be an expert on the Bible or a trained teacher to lead a Bible discussion. The idea behind these inductive studies is that the leader guides group members to discover for themselves what the Bible has to say. This method of learning will allow group members to remember much more of what is said than a lecture would.

These studies are designed to be led easily. As a matter of fact, the flow of questions through the passage from observation to interpretation to application is so natural that you may feel that the studies lead themselves. This study guide is also flexible. You can use it with a variety of groups—student, professional, neighborhood or church groups. Each study takes forty-five to sixty minutes in a group setting.

There are some important facts to know about group dynamics and encouraging discussion. The suggestions listed below should enable you to effectively and enjoyably fulfill your role as leader.

Preparing for the Study

1. Ask God to help you understand and apply the passage in your own life. Unless this happens, you will not be prepared to lead others. Pray too for the various members of the group. Ask God to open your hearts to the message of his Word and motivate you to action.

2. Read the introduction to the entire guide to get an overview of the entire book and the issues which will be explored.

3. As you begin each study, read and reread the assigned Bible passage to familiarize yourself with it.

4. This study guide is based on the New International Version of the Bible. It will help you and the group if you use this translation as the basis for your study and discussion.

5. Carefully work through each question in the study. Spend time in meditation and reflection as you consider how to respond.

6. Write your thoughts and responses in the space provided in the study guide. This will help you to express your understanding of the passage clearly.

7. It might help to have a Bible dictionary handy. Use it to look up any unfamiliar words, names or places. (For additional help on how to study a passage, see chapter five of *How to Lead a LifeGuide Bible Study*, InterVarsity Press.)

8. Consider how you can apply the Scripture to your life. Remember that the group will follow your lead in responding to the studies. They will not go any deeper than you do.

9. Once you have finished your own study of the passage, familiarize yourself with the leader's notes for the study you are leading. These are designed to help you in several ways. First, they tell you the purpose the study guide author had in mind when writing the study. Take time to think through how the study questions work together to accomplish that purpose. Second, the notes provide you with additional background information or suggestions on group dynamics for various questions. This information can be useful when people have difficulty understanding or answering a question. Third, the leader's notes can alert you to potential problems you may encounter during the study.

10. If you wish to remind yourself of anything mentioned in the leader's notes, make a note to yourself below that question in the study.

Leading the Study

1. Begin the study on time. Open with prayer, asking God to help the group to understand and apply the passage.

2. Be sure that everyone in your group has a study guide. Encourage the group to prepare beforehand for each discussion by reading the introduction to the guide and by working through the questions in the study.

3. At the beginning of your first time together, explain that these studies are meant to be discussions, not lectures. Encourage the members of the group to participate. However, do not put pressure on those who may be hesitant to speak during the first few sessions. You may want to suggest the following guidelines to your group.

■ Stick to the topic being discussed.

■ Your responses should be based on the verses which are the focus of the discussion and not on outside authorities such as commentaries or speakers.
■ These studies focus on a particular passage of Scripture. Only rarely should you refer to other portions of the Bible. This allows for everyone to participate in in-depth study on equal ground.
■ Anything said in the group is considered confidential and will not be discussed outside the group unless specific permission is given to do so.
■ We will listen attentively to each other and provide time for each person present to talk.
■ We will pray for each other.

4. Have a group member read the introduction at the beginning of the discussion.

5. Every session begins with a group discussion question. The question or activity is meant to be used before the passage is read. The question introduces the theme of the study and encourages group members to begin to open up. Encourage as many members as possible to participate, and be ready to get the discussion going with your own response.

This section is designed to reveal where our thoughts or feelings need to be transformed by Scripture. That is why it is especially important not to read the passage before the discussion question is asked. The passage will tend to color the honest reactions people would otherwise give because they are, of course, supposed to think the way the Bible does.

You may want to supplement the group discussion question with an icebreaker to help people to get comfortable. See the community section of *Small Group Idea Book* for more ideas.

You also might want to use the personal reflection question with your group. Either allow a time of silence for people to respond individually or discuss it together.

6. Have a group member (or members if the passage is long) read aloud the passage to be studied. Then give people several minutes to read the passage again silently so that they can take it all in.

7. Question 1 will generally be an overview question designed to briefly survey the passage. Encourage the group to look at the whole passage, but try to avoid getting sidetracked by questions or issues that will be addressed later in the study.

8. As you ask the questions, keep in mind that they are designed to be used just as they are written. You may simply read them aloud. Or you may prefer to express them in your own words.

There may be times when it is appropriate to deviate from the study guide.

For example, a question may have already been answered. If so, move on to the next question. Or someone may raise an important question not covered in the guide. Take time to discuss it, but try to keep the group from going off on tangents.

9. Avoid answering your own questions. If necessary, repeat or rephrase them until they are clearly understood. Or point out something you read in the leader's notes to clarify the context or meaning. An eager group quickly becomes passive and silent if they think the leader will do most of the talking.

10. Don't be afraid of silence. People may need time to think about the question before formulating their answers.

11. Don't be content with just one answer. Ask, "What do the rest of you think?" or "Anything else?" until several people have given answers to the question.

12. Acknowledge all contributions. Try to be affirming whenever possible. Never reject an answer. If it is clearly off-base, ask, "Which verse led you to that conclusion?" or again, "What do the rest of you think?"

13. Don't expect every answer to be addressed to you, even though this will probably happen at first. As group members become more at ease, they will begin to truly interact with each other. This is one sign of healthy discussion.

14. Don't be afraid of controversy. It can be very stimulating. If you don't resolve an issue completely, don't be frustrated. Move on and keep it in mind for later. A subsequent study may solve the problem.

15. Periodically summarize what the group has said about the passage. This helps to draw together the various ideas mentioned and gives continuity to the study. But don't preach.

16. At the end of the Bible discussion you may want to allow group members a time of quiet to work on an idea under "Now or Later." Then discuss what you experienced. Or you may want to encourage group members to work on these ideas between meetings. Give an opportunity during the session for people to talk about what they are learning.

17. Conclude your time together with conversational prayer, adapting the prayer suggestion at the end of the study to your group. Ask for God's help in following through on the commitments you've made.

18. End on time.

Many more suggestions and helps are found in *How to Lead a LifeGuide Bible Study*.

Components of Small Groups
A healthy small group should do more than study the Bible. There are four

components to consider as you structure your time together.

Nurture. Small groups help us to grow in our knowledge and love of God. Bible study is the key to making this happen and is the foundation of your small group.

Community. Small groups are a great place to develop deep friendships with other Christians. Allow time for informal interaction before and after each study. Plan activities and games that will help you get to know each other. Spend time having fun together—going on a picnic or cooking dinner together.

Worship and prayer. Your study will be enhanced by spending time praising God together in prayer or song. Pray for each other's needs—and keep track of how God is answering prayer in your group. Ask God to help you to apply what you are learning in your study.

Outreach. Reaching out to others can be a practical way of applying what you are learning, and it will keep your group from becoming self-focused. Host a series of evangelistic discussions for your friends or neighbors. Clean up the yard of an elderly friend. Serve at a soup kitchen together, or spend a day working on a Habitat house.

Many more suggestions and helps in each of these areas are found in *Small Group Idea Book.* Information on building a small group can be found in *Small Group Leaders' Handbook* and *The Big Book on Small Groups* (both from Inter-Varsity Press). Reading through one of these books would be worth your time.

Study 1. The Last Days Are Here! Acts 2.

Purpose: To explore the lifestyle challenge of living in the age inaugurated by the ascension of Jesus and the outpouring of the Spirit.

Question 1. The later occurrences of the gift of tongues (Acts 8:17-18; 10:46-47; 11:17; 19:6) are probably a direct extension of this supernatural endowment as new frontiers were broken in the crosscultural mission of the church, in contrast to the Corinthian tongues, which required interpretation (1 Cor 14:2, 27). Taking the occurrences of *glossolalia* (tongues) in Acts together, it appears that God wanted to convince the disciples *experientially* that their vocation was now to share in the worldwide mission of Christ by empowering them to speak foreign languages and dialects they had never learned. There is in this a possible allusion to a Jewish tradition that at the giving of the Law the voice of God was heard in every nation under heaven, then considered to be seventy in all (F. F. Bruce, *The Acts of the Apostles* [London: Tyndale Press, 1965], p. 83). That the Jerusalem event was clearly a supernatural phenomenon is evidenced by the jeer of the cynical bystanders. Later, missionaries had to learn some of those languages.

Question 2. In contrast to the breakdown of communication at Babel (Gen 11:1-9), the Spirit empowers the disciples to experience community of speech.

The three great festivals of Israel at the time of Jesus were Passover (remembering deliverance from Egypt), Tabernacles (recalling the wilderness wanderings) and Pentecost (a harvest festival coming seven weeks after Passover, during which the first fruits were offered to God—Ex 23:16; Lev 23:15-21). Sometimes over a million people jammed into Jerusalem for these festivals, arriving from all over the Mediterranean (from modern Italy to Egypt). Many of the visitors were Jews in dispersion. Some were proselytes (Gentiles who had become Jews by baptism and circumcision). Some were God-fearers (non-Jews who were earnestly seeking God—see Zech 8:23). It was an auspicious occasion for the missionary vocation of the church to be sealed, and for the first harvests of Christ's resurrection and ascension to be made. Significantly, the apostle Paul later chose the feast of Pentecost to bring the love-gift from the Gentile churches to the Jewish believers in Palestine (Acts 20:16) in the true spirit of the international, interracial community born that day, anticipating as Paul said "the full measure of the blessing of Christ" (Rom 15:29).

Speaking to Jews and proselytes, Peter declares the finality of Jesus by quoting psalms that envisioned a triumph over death by God's anointed messenger and the ascension by the Messiah to rule over everything at God's right hand. It is not surprising that at least some of Peter's audience were "cut to the heart" by this revelation as they realized they had unwittingly participated in the murder of God's anointed One, even though they may have believed at the time they were doing God's will in eliminating who they believed was an imposter and a blasphemer. What is surprising and troubling is the apathetic response of people today to the same message. Noteworthy and helpful to us in our mission is the way Peter addresses the need of the people to believe by appealing to Scripture, to the facts of the crucifixion and the empty tomb, and to the supernatural phenomenon of Pentecost, evidences that carry weight even today.

Question 4. John Stott takes this passage and carefully outlines what the events of Pentecost were *not:* (1) not the result of intoxication, (2) not a miracle in hearing, in contrast to speaking, (3) not a case of incoherent speech. Rather, "the *glossolalia* on the Day of Pentecost was a supernatural ability to speak in recognizable languages." Stott carefully shows the multifaceted reality of Pentecost as (1) a final unrepeatable act in the saving ministry of Jesus; (2) the empowerment of the apostles for their unique role; (3) the inauguration of the new era of the Spirit—so that Pentecost gets extended through history; and (4) the first revival in the church. He wisely concludes, "The wind and fire were abnormal, and probably the languages too; the new life and joy, fellowship and worship, freedom, boldness and power were not" (*The Spirit, the Church and the World* [Downers Grove, Ill.: InterVarsity Press, 1990], pp. 60-61, 65-66).

Questions 5-6. Two things are noteworthy in the fulfillment of Joel's prophecy. First, Old Testament prophets were more concerned with holiness in time than holiness in space: the day of the Lord was more important than the house of the Lord. But the day is not to be calculated on a clock or a calendar. It is God's own time—a season extending, as we now know, through centuries. Second, two dimensions of the day (grace and judgment) locked together in Joel's prophecy are separated at least temporarily in Christian fulfillment. The day *now* is a day of opportunity to experience new life, forgiveness and the full endowment of the Spirit. But it will *eventually* mean final irrevocable judgment for the obstinate and unbelieving. Our detailed study of Joel will show this.

Question 7. While some might prefer to debate the relative merits of infant and adult-believer's baptism, it is advisable to focus on the issues raised by this first generation of new Christians in this missionary situation. There is some question as to the relationship between the baptism mentioned in this passage and two other baptisms—John's baptism of repentance and the baptism of Gentile converts to Judaism. It is uncertain when Jewish baptism of proselytes began, so John's baptism may or may not have been modeled after Jewish tradition. Although there could be a connection to the ritual daily cleansing prevalent in Jewish law, both the baptism after Pentecost and John's baptism were one-time events reflecting an inner change in a person's life, not the daily need for repurification.

Question 8. Whether Paul thought there would be a fresh outpouring of the Holy Spirit on the day of Pentecost when he presented the huge love-gift from the Gentile believers to the Jewish believers, he must have seen the significance as entering into the true meaning of Pentecost and so pressed his travel schedule to get to Jerusalem in time for the feast (Acts 20:16). See also "Now or Later."

Question 10. Though the temporary experiment in what has been called "a religious communism of love" had a disastrous moment (Acts 5:1-11), and was soon transformed into almsgiving (4:1-7) and relief missions (11:27-30; Rom 15:25-28), a crucial principle is demonstrated: fellowship is more than "spiritual" sharing. During the period before the persecution and scattering of the Jerusalem Christians (Acts 8:1-3) and the destruction of the temple in A.D. 70, these first believers participated in sanctuary worship with other Jews and a new form of home fellowship distinctive of the new life Jesus brought. It was said of early Christians that they shared a common table but not a common bed, thus redeeming and redefining the word for love in the ancient world and making their life together a sermon. A last-days lifestyle is neither superspiritual nor impractical. This winsome community that attracted outsiders (Acts 2:47) was authenticated by Spirit-endowed preaching, a radical life of practical love, and wonders and signs (2:43).

Study 2. He Will Come Back. John 14:1-27.

Purpose: To explore the relevance of our present experience of the Holy Spirit to the process of waiting for the Second Coming of Jesus.

Question 1. Remarkably Jesus stresses the ministry of preparing heaven for us rather than merely preparing us for heaven!

The meaning of *monai* ("rooms," v. 2) is not entirely clear. While some have translated this "mansions" or "resting places," it appears from the context that permanent abodes are meant. As Leon Morris says, "The idea of continuing development in the next world, though attractive and possibly true, is not taught in Scripture" (Leon Morris, *The Gospel According to John*, NICNT [Grand Rapids, Mich.: Eerdmans, 1971], p. 638). While nothing is said about the nature of the place being prepared, it is enough to know that the believer will be with Jesus. In this passage "where" gives way to "how" and ultimately to "who." Even the Second Coming, which has a lesser place in the fourth Gospel in comparison to the others, is presented in these personal, Christ-centered terms: Christ must come again to take us to our ultimate home.

Question 3. In John 13 Peter has just heard that he will deny the Lord three times. A great trial is imminent. And now Jesus is speaking of his departure. They have left everything to follow him and now he is leaving them. So Jesus is not speaking to people who are untroubled, but rather to those racked with anxiety. The reasons for faith offered in this chapter are not merely rational but include their experience of the Spirit, who will be given when Jesus leaves. So great is this coming assurance that Jesus dares to say, "If you loved me, you would be glad that I am going to the Father, for the Father is greater than I" (Jn 14:28).

Question 5. Often the claims of Jesus to *be* the way (and not merely to show the way), to *be* the truth, and to *be* the life are taken to be exclusionary, and Christians are criticized for their bigoted claims. However, it is important to note that it is Jesus who makes these claims for himself and not merely Christians who are making statements about their religion. In contrast to the claims of religious leaders who offer hope and blessing for the spiritually enlightened, Jesus offers relationship with himself as an all-sufficient way that could potentially include everyone. Philip's question (14:8) is a veiled request for a revelation of God such as occurred occasionally in the Old Testament (Ex 24:10; 33:17; Is 6:1). Jesus' answer is that the Father and the Son live in such mutual interpenetration that Jesus is truly the full and final revelation of the Father. To see Jesus is to see the Father (Jn 1:18; 12:45; 13:20). As Leon Morris says, "Faith that there is a mutual indwelling of the Father and the Son is part of the faith whereby a man commits himself to Christ. If there is no such indwelling there can scarcely be full commitment" (Morris, *Gospel*, p. 645).

Question 7. This question has led many scholars to argue that for John's audience, now discouraged that Christ has not come back soon after his ascension, the real hope is their present experience of the Holy Spirit. This is the Second Coming. And in a limited sense this view is partly correct. As "another" paraclete (meaning comforter or legal friend), the Holy Spirit is, as it were, another Jesus to the disciples. In John's Gospel the Spirit is closely linked with the work of Jesus—making Jesus present and interpreting his words. The Spirit is the presence of Jesus when Jesus is absent. C. K. Barrett says, "The Spirit's work is to bear witness to Christ [and] to make operative what Christ had already effected. The Spirit is thus the eschatological continuum in which the work of Christ, initiated in his ministry and awaiting its termination at his return, is wrought out" (quoted in Gary M. Burge, *The Anointed Community: The Holy Spirit in the Johannine Tradition* [Grand Rapids, Mich.: Eerdmans, 1987], pp. 83-84). The coming of the Holy Spirit continues and completes the ministry of Jesus. This is expressed in the five sayings of the Spirit in John: (1) "he lives with you and will be in you" (14:16-17); (2) he "will teach you all things" (14:26); (3) "he will testify about me" (15:26); (4) "he will convict the world of guilt in regard to sin and righteousness and judgment" (16:7-11); and (5) "he will guide you into all truth" (16:13-15). But to the question "Is the paraclete in fact Jesus returned?" we must answer no, even if only John's Gospel were considered. Jesus' use of the words *going* and *coming* have a double reference: to the coming of the eschatological Spirit, and to his final coming in glory.

Question 8. This is the only use of *monē* ("room") other than verse 2. And here it is reinterpreted to point not to a heavenly dwelling but to a *present indwelling* of the Father and the Son in the believer through the Spirit (v. 17). As Gary Burge shows, Judas's question in verse 22 points to the expectation of a personal, visible return of Christ in the clouds so that every eye will see him. "But John 14 presents a new definition. Jesus' personal indwelling along with the Father (vv. 23-24) will be Judas's own personal epiphany" (*Anointed Community*, p. 144).

Question 9. John's special contribution to living in the end times is this double "coming" of Jesus, first in the Spirit, who is in a real sense Jesus come back. Indeed, while the disciples might have been satisfied with fellowship with Jesus alone, it would not be possible to have a permanent indwelling of Jesus without the coming of the Spirit (Jn 20:22). From our postascension perspective one cannot be a Christian without an encounter with the dynamic Spirit. But the second meaning of "coming" points to Christ's final coming that is suggested when Jesus speaks of "my Father's house" (14:2) and promises to take the disciples to be with him (14:3). Having the Spirit is even better than having Jesus in the flesh. And having Christ come again visibly and finally in history is best of all!

Study 3. Signs of the Times. Mark 13.
Purpose: To show how fulfilled promises made by Jesus inspire our watchfulness for the greatest promise of all—the promise that Jesus will come back in glory to receive his own.
General note. In his farewell address on the Mount of Olives overlooking Jerusalem, Jesus was pointing to events that would happen in the future and instructing his disciples on how they were to live when he would no longer be with them.
Question 1. Malachi 3:1-6 describes the coming of the Lord to purify and refine his rebellious people. This was fulfilled in the events prophesied by Jesus. The background of this passage is the destruction of the temple in Jerusalem in A.D. 70 by the Roman emperor Titus in response to Jewish insurrection, a literal fulfillment of prophecy. But at the time of the writing of Mark this event had not happened. So this prophecy and its warnings had immediate urgency for the first generation of believers about to enter a tumultuous period of history. As we shall see, it also has great significance for us long after the prophecy of the destruction of the temple was fulfilled. While the first readers of the Gospel were asked to trust the eternal word of Jesus (13:31) concerning two future events—(1) the destruction of the temple and the surrounding disorders, and (2) the coming of the Son of Man to consummate the new temple of his people—we have the privilege of being able to trust the God who fulfilled the first prophecy as we wait for the fulfillment of the second.
Questions 3-4. "In those days" (v. 24) is an expression from the Old Testament normally associated with last times. The "Son of Man" is the chosen title of Jesus for himself, drawn from the figure of a supernatural person in Daniel 7:13 who receives the worship of *all* nations. Jesus speaks of his Second Coming in a personal, visible and triumphant manner in terms of the coming of the Son of Man.

This section of Old Testament imagery is expressed in a form of literature called *apocalyptic,* meaning "to unveil." Mark 13 is sometimes called "the little apocalypse" because of its similarity to the last book of the Bible, which bears the name Apocalypse, or Revelation. Apocalypse is a lost literary genre in modern Western Christianity. Apocalypse was to the first century what science fiction is to the twentieth. Apocalypse is a form of revelatory literature in which cosmic upheavals affecting the sun and moon signal the intervention of God in history. The coming of the Son of Man "with the clouds" signals the end of the veiledness we presently experience in our relation to God and his purposes. Here Jesus (who claimed to be greater than the temple) uses the coming destruction of the temple—the visible center of the gathered chosen people—to speak of the eventual replacement of the temple by the Son of Man surrounded by his reconstituted people from all nations. The apocalyptic form of speech calls for radical discipleship.

The "abomination that causes desolation" alludes to Daniel 9:27 and 11:31, and it refers to the desecration of the temple in Jerusalem by a profane person or a profane object that makes necessary the abandonment of the temple as a place of worship by the people of God. The most likely fulfillment of this prophecy happened in the events of A.D. 67-68 when Jewish fanatics occupied the temple area and allowed people who had committed crimes to roam freely in the holy of holies—even those who had committed murder within the temple precincts. This sacrilege climaxed in the insane appointment of the clown Phanni as high priest. Jewish Christians were still worshiping daily within the temple precincts and, in response to this prophecy of Jesus, fled across the Jordan to the Transjordan hills and found refuge in Pella. A second fulfillment to the prophecy occurred on August 30, A.D. 70, when the temple was captured by the Romans and set on fire. Titus, the Roman general, entered the holy of holies and erected the Roman military standards. Soon fire and destruction led to "not one stone . . . left on another, every one . . . thrown down" (13:2). These events happened in the lifetime of the first disciples.

Question 5. William Lane notes that the nineteen imperatives found in verses 5-37 suggest that "the primary function of chapter 13 is not to disclose esoteric information but to promote faith and obedience in a time of distress and upheaval" (William L. Lane, *Commentary on the Gospel of Mark,* NICNT [Grand Rapids, Mich.: Eerdmans, 1974], p. 446).

While the words of Jesus concerning the stresses ahead were literally fulfilled in the lifetime of the first disciples, they offer stark realism about the difficulty believers will face in every generation. The world will not get better and better before the Lord comes. The Christian life will never be easy.

Believers will experience rejection because they are associated with Jesus. The "birthpangs of the Messiah" is a favorite Old Testament theme of judgment (Is 13:8; 26:17; Jer 4:31; 6:24; 50:43; Hos 13:13; Mic 4:9). The statement that these religious, social, personal, familial and natural disasters are only the beginning of the travail (13:8) suggests that the second fulfillment of the passage (the appearance of the Lord Jesus in triumph) might be long delayed. In the meantime the disciples will proclaim the gospel to all humankind (13:10), a crucial end-times activity that will not be impeded by social disruption or persecution.

Question 7. The vision of people from the ends of the earth gathering around Jesus (v. 27) is related to the proclamation of the gospel to all people (v. 10). Both the coming of the Son of Man and the preaching of the gospel to all nations are end-times events.

Question 8. It should now be clear that verses 30 and 32 relate to two distinct events, the first of which Jesus is sure will happen in the generation of the first disciples, and the second of which even he does not know the exact date or time. The parable of vigilance would apply to Jesus' first disciples and to both events. To us it applies only to the second. Mark has taken the original words of Jesus on the Mount of Olives and applied them to his readers then and now. One remarkable feature of this parable, which is found only in Mark, is that though members of the household had different works to perform while they were waiting—and one even to stand at the door—all were required to be vigilant. Even hard times (13:8) are not a sure sign that he will come immediately! One reason to hold lightly to our own confidence that the end is near is this strange fact: the apostle Paul believed that the gospel had been fully proclaimed to the world within his own lifetime (Rom 10:18; Col 1:6), as we believe is uniquely possible now within our own lifetimes (Paul Barnett, *The Servant King: Reading Mark Today* [Sydney: Anglican Information Office, 1991], p. 250).

Those who doubt that Jesus will return would do well to reflect that the sign of his coming, the destruction of the temple, took place as he said it would. *All* other prophecies of Jesus—his death and resurrection, the coming of the Holy Spirit, the persecution of his followers, the rise of the Jewish "sign" prophets, the desecration and destruction of the temple, and the sufferings in Judea—have been fulfilled in history. Only his prophecy of the Second Coming awaits historical fulfillment (Barnett, *Servant King*, 254).

Study 4. Grappling with Radical Evil. 2 Thessalonians 2.
Purpose: To learn how to stand firm during times when we encounter almost overwhelming evil in society.

Question 1. In 1 Thessalonians, a very early letter in the New Testament, Paul lets us see into the life of a newly planted church (see Acts 17). But 2 Thessalonians is Paul's response to the disturbing news he receives while in Corinth about the church in Thessalonica. Heavy persecution has broken out, and the people are wondering why God allows his people to suffer and what will be the end of it all. Further, false teachers are saying that the day of the Lord has already come, and this message, from a document that claimed to be from Paul himself, was being circulated. It is not only persecutors from outside that are harassing the believers but false teachers *inside*. Finally, some people have given up working entirely and were merely "waiting" for the end. As John Stott says, "Paul sets the current problems of the Thessalonian church firmly in the context of the historical process and its climax when Christ comes" (*The Gospel and the End of Time: The Message of 1 & 2 Thessalonians* [Downers Grove, Ill.: InterVarsity Press, 1991], p. 21).

Questions 2 and 4. Undoubtedly the apparent delay in the Lord's coming had promoted concern for those who had already died (a subject Paul explores in 1 Thess 4:13). Added to this was the false teaching that Christ had already come, a teaching promoted in our own day by the Jehovah's Witnesses and by those who hold a fully "realized eschatology" (the end has fully come, and we have Christ's complete eternal life now). Paul responds by indicating that the Lord cannot return until both an event occurs and a person appears. Both the "rebellion"—a great apostasy and final revolt against God—and the "man of lawlessness"—a person embodying that final rebellion—will be explored in this study.

In our study of Mark 13:14 we encountered "the abomination that causes desolation" (a gross and blasphemous desecration of the physical temple in Jerusalem), a prophecy that was fulfilled in the first generation of believers. But here Paul appears to broaden this concept, drawn largely from Daniel, and applies it to a *principle* of rebellion that will be at work through history—whether that history is long or short—and a *person* who embodies that full and final revolt against God. While Paul does not use the word John does for that person—the antichrist (1 Jn 2:18)—he is apparently referring to the same thing. In 2 Thessalonians Paul uses four titles for this person: the antinomian (lawless one who is defiant of all law; see Mt 24:12), the doomed, the enemy and the God-pretender. John Stott notes that the two principal targets of this man are ethics and religion.

Many people struggle as they try to identify this enigmatic figure because of the reference to setting himself up in God's temple (v. 4). Preliminary manifestations of the antichrist in the temple during the Jewish war of A.D. 66-70 were explored in the last study. But here, in the context of the global empire of the antichrist, it appears that the temple reference is a motif, or a metaphorical expression indicating his infiltration of Christendom. In the Revelation this principle finds expression in the figure of the two beasts (Rev 13) exemplified in the arrogant Roman emperor Domitian who claimed to be a god, and the imperial cult that required even Christians to offer their sacrifices to the emperor as divine. Neither 2 Thessalonians nor Revelation find their complete fulfillment in the first century but point to multiple fulfillments in both political and religious leaders throughout the history of the church. (See John Stott's masterful summary of this in *Gospel and the End of Time*, pp. 159-67.) That, however, does not preclude a final and ultimate manifestation of the antichrist in a concrete historical person immediately prior to the Second Coming. Indeed, as John Stott says, "whether we still believe in the coming of antichrist will depend largely on whether we will believe in the coming of Christ" (*Gospel and the End of Time*, p. 167). Turning it around, not to believe in the Second Coming of Christ would lead to an unthinkable future when the rebellion finally happens and the antichrist is fully revealed.

Question 5. Paul notes that lawlessness and spiritual seduction are already at work but are being held back. Identifying this restraining power has been one of the riddles of biblical interpretation throughout history. Candidates that have been suggested are (1) the Holy Spirit and the work of the church, (2) Paul and the preaching of the gospel, and (3) Rome and the power of the state in succeeding generations. If, as John Stott and others propose, the third is the most likely alternative, the complexity (the "mystery") of evil is even more apparent: the state, which in Romans 13 and 2 Thessalonians is the church's protector by providing law and order, becomes in Revelation 13 the church's enemy articulated directly by Satan himself. In any event, the "mystery" of the rebellion and the lawless one are operating in a subtle, underground way discernable only to the eye of faith. While it appears that culture and ideology in our self-fulfilling society offer freedom from restraints and unbridled pursuit of pleasure, they would soon destroy us utterly but for the restraints imposed. The ultimate restraint will be the coming of the Lord Jesus when the escalated moral, social, political and spiritual chaos will be decisively and finally overcome.

Questions 6. Here the work and parousia (appearing, 2:9) of Satan is presented as a parody of the parousia of Jesus in several dimensions so that people unfortified by the apostle's teaching (2:10) can easily be led astray by the counterfeit presence, appearance and miraculous works of the antichrist. One is reminded of Paul's later statement that even Satan comes as an attractive angel of light (2 Cor 11:14). While the direct cause of the deepening delusion (2:11) that overwhelms these would-be or one-time believers is God himself, it is one more case of the frequently repeated scriptural principle that continuously rejecting the truth leads ultimately to the incapacity of discerning truth from error at all. This is parallel to the self-chosen delusion of those who experience the wrath of God (Rom 1:24, 26, 28) because they failed to embrace the truth of God. The way to be protected from this grim descent to hell (delighting in wickedness, refusing to believe, being deceived and then being totally deluded) is to love goodness and truth, which is implicit in loving God with mind, heart and soul.

Question 7. James Denney called 2:13-14 "a system of theology in miniature" since it points to the protecting power of all three persons of the Trinity and emphasizes God's initiative in both accomplishing our salvation and maintaining us in our saved state. Thanksgiving (humble, grateful dependence on God and continuous appreciation of his goodness) and holding to sound teaching (humble, grateful dependence on God's saving Word and continuous appreciation of the goodness of the Word of Christ delivered by the apostles—and now contained in Scripture) are two anchors for the soul. Believers can face the mounting pressures and storms without panic or unnecessary apprehension.

Paul's final prayer (2:16-17) for the encouragement of his friends is based on certainty of the "eternal encouragement" of God himself. Far from inspiring passivity, this knowledge of God's gracious previousness and persistent encouragement give "good hope" to the heart no matter what the immediate future might bring, a hope of eternity expressed not only in word but in deed. Fundamental to this is our experience of the love of God (2:13, 16; 3:5), a "love that wilt not let me go."

Study 5. God's Timing—and Ours. Joel 2:12-32.

Purpose: To show how understanding the day of the Lord can bring joyful gratitude to the fulfillment we presently experience in Christ, and joyful anticipation of more to come.

Questions 1-2. It seems impossible to date Joel's prophecies more accurately than to place them somewhere between the eighth and the fourth century before Christ. Joel was drawing on the heritage of previous prophets about the day of the Lord, a day when God would intervene in history to redeem his own people. The first mention of that day (Amos 5:18-20; 9:7-8) takes an important turn—even the Lord's people may experience judgment on that day! Zephaniah also taught that the day of the Lord would simultaneously be a threat to the compromised chosen people (1:1—2:3) and the foreign nations ripe for judgment (2:4-15). In line with Obadiah, who believed the day had come, Joel sees in the plague of locusts a preliminary manifestation of that day. Judgment had come *first* to God's household (1 Pet 4:17). It is the "now" (v. 12) of God's timing. If they respond appropriately, God's people will face a blissful future untroubled by the terror to be experienced by the rest of the nations. The difference between the Lord's people and the other nations is the covenant relationship (he is *your* God), which is presupposed in the call to repentance. As Leslie Allen says, "The prophets often presuppose that the proclamation and inauguration of punishment for God's people are interim, *ad hoc* measures, closely related to the present state of their hearts and lives" (*The Books of Joel, Obadiah, Jonah and Micah* [Grand Rapids, Mich.: Eerdmans, 1976], p. 78).

Question 4. In the Bible *covenant* is the term that describes the binding personal relationship between God and this one chosen people as exemplified in the oft-repeated formula "I am your God and you are my people." Israel was unique in the ancient world as having its national identity formed by a covenant made with a single deity. What makes this judgment passage so poignant and at the same time so hopeful is the fact that it concerns God's own covenant people. In the context of assuring them of mighty acts of blessing from God upon condition of their repentance, Joel pictures the bountiful return of the basics: grain, wine and oil.

The reference in verse 20 to "the northern army" points to the horde of locusts which the Lord will drive away, a horde now treated in a more figurative manner in line with the apocalyptic hordes of Gog from the north bent on destroying Judah (Ezek 38:15; 39:2). The bad years (v. 25) will be more than compensated by the good years to come. Experiencing the curses of the covenant is expressed in terms of deprivation of life in this world. In the same way the restoration of covenant harmony must have a this-worldly manifestation as evidence that God really dwells with his people (v. 27).

Questions 5-6. As a deeper indication of covenant fulfillment and evidence of the Lord's presence with his people, Joel prophesies a Spirit outpouring as a counterpart to the outpouring of rain (2:23). There are three dimensions of supernatural blessings: Spirit presence (vv. 28-29), signs of Spirit power (vv. 30-31) and ultimate security (v. 32). In the first (2:28-29) of the three dimensions, Joel envisions a universal ministry of prophecy (direct and immediate speech and visions from God) that includes men and women, old and young, and even slaves. The supernatural signs are standard figurative terms used in end-times passages in both testaments (Is 13:10, 13; 34:2-4, 10; Ezek 32:3-8; Amos 8:9; Rev 6:12). These "supercharged" images of creation undergoing change express the truth that things can never be the same again. In contrast to the nations for whom the day holds only judgment (3:1-16), the Lord's people can find security in God's home, Mount Zion in Jerusalem, an image that is taken up in the New Testament.

Question 7. Under the Old Covenant direct messages from God were rare (1 Sam 3:1) and restricted almost completely to the prophets and sages. Joel's vision of community-wide ministry of the Word of God is consistent with other prophesies (see also Is 54:13; Jer 31:31-40; Ezek 39:29). It is apparent, however, that Joel did not envision an outpouring *beyond* Israel. Neither did Peter. Even though Peter quoted this passage on the day of Pentecost, he was truly amazed later when another unthinkable frontier was passed: even the Gentiles could become Spirit people (Acts 10:45).

Questions 8-9. The concept of the day of the Lord in the Old Testament centered on the truth of God's saving judgment as he enters history. It was prefigured by the plagues of Egypt (literally, the "strokes" of God's judgment), which simultaneously brought judgment on the Egyptians and salvation to the believing Hebrews. As mentioned above, the various dimensions of the day of the Lord are like distant mountain peaks that form a tableau with undefined distances between the peaks. The order does not seem to matter ultimately once one encounters God's time.

So in Joel's prophecy the day included relief from judgment for God's own penitent people evidenced in both material and spiritual blessing, while outsiders could anticipate only the terror of unrelieved judgment. Under the more complete fulfillment of the day surrounding the coming of Christ the order gets somewhat reversed: final judgment is delayed, while the immediate spiritual blessings of universal Spirit-endowed language become a reason to repent and be baptized (Acts 2:38) rather than a consequence of the people's repentance. Signs of supernatural power had already been demonstrated in the miracles of Jesus and were perpetuated by the first believers (Acts 2:43). A further irony is that Peter urges separation from "this crooked generation" (2:40)—referring to Jews unwilling to accept Christ—and suggests through his use of Psalm 110:1 that the crushing defeat formerly reserved for the enemies of God and Israel can be experienced by people who are nominally God's people (Jews) though not spiritually so.

Later still, Paul quotes Joel 2:32 in Romans 10:13 to prove that the gracious provision of the *saving* aspect of God's judgment during the day of the Lord includes even Gentiles who are equally positioned to receive the grace of God in Christ. Empowered by the vision of the exalted Christ and the Gentile-embracing gospel, Paul went into the Gentile world to preach the grace of the day of the Lord, pleading with non-Jews (Acts 17:31) to repent before the final day of judgment. Under apostolic preaching the full material blessings of covenant restoration and fulfillment wait for the new heaven and the new earth (Rev 21—22).

So the seed of Joel's prophecy finds multiple fulfillments in clock-time sequences that appear from our perspective to be different from the original plan, while being fulfilled in ways that even Joel could not have dreamed. Indeed, there was *no plan.* There was in Joel's prophecy an eschatological (end times) vision that would be largely fulfilled in Christ's first coming when the church was born. But it would be ultimately fulfilled (in the same way that fruit is more than seed) when Christ will come again. Meanwhile God's time penetrates seasons and clock and calendar time until time itself will be fully transformed, along with the rest of the cosmos.

Study 6. The Future of the Human Person. 1 Corinthians 15:12-28, 35-44, 58.
Purpose: To show how the promise of resurrection with Christ makes life in our present bodies meaningful and important.
General note. The theologian Oscar Cullmann outlines the Greek view that profoundly influenced the Corinthians, as it does people in the West: "The soul, confined within the body, belongs to the eternal world. As long as we live, our soul finds itself in a prison, that is, in a body essentially alien to it" (*Immortality of the Soul or Resurrection of the Dead? The Witness of the New Testament* [London: Epworth, 1958], pp. 19-20). Cullmann compares the romantic notion of the "beautiful" death of the Greek philosopher Socrates with the fearful and awful death of Jesus and concludes that, for Christian and Jewish thinking, death is the destruction of God-created life. Death is not beautiful, not even the death of Jesus.
Question 1. The most likely reason reflects the conflict that runs through the whole Corinthian correspondence, namely that by receiving the Spirit and especially by receiving the gift of tongues the Corinthians thought they had already entered the ultimate spiritual state (4:8), a form of angelic existence (4:9; 13:1) in which the body would be unnecessary and therefore destroyed. "Thus for them life in the Spirit meant a final ridding oneself of the body, not because it was evil but because it was inferior and beneath them" (Gordon D. Fee, *The First Epistle to the Corinthians,* NICNT [Grand Rapids, Mich.: Eerdmans, 1987], p. 715). The idea that the body would be raised would have been unthinkable. Further, Fee offers that the strange practice of the Corinthians of baptizing for the dead (15:29) may also relate to their offering to the dead an exalted spiri-

tual existence similar to what they claimed already to have. Christ's own resurrection is the prototype and the pledge for the rest of us. For the apostle Paul the resurrection of Jesus bodily from the grave is the ultimate end-times event through which God overthrew the tyranny of death and guaranteed our own resurrection. Our future is not to be a disembodied soul floating through eternity but a fully human person, equipped with a resurrected body.

Questions 4-5. This is not an easy verse (v. 19) to translate or to understand. The problem is to determine what the "only" modifies—whether "this life" or "hope." However, Paul's positive use of "hope" throughout the letter demands the former, namely that having Christ now without a certain future would make us pitiable. As Gordon Fee points out, however, generations of Christians have taken this (correct translation) the wrong way and argued that Christian faith is interested *only* in the future, thereby devaluing our present existence. In fact this statement is made in the context of the argument that if Christ is not raised from the dead we have lost not only our present forgiveness (v. 17) but also our hope for the future. (Fee, *First Epistle,* p. 745).

Question 6. This section gives a comprehensive overview of the work of Christ at the "end time." As we have seen over and over again in our studies, events are not laid out in a fixed sequence but presented in tableau fashion. Further, as we have seen, end-times events began with the death and resurrection of Christ (the beginning on the day of the Lord) and finish with the Second Coming of Christ (the completion of the day of the Lord) and all the realities associated with that glorious consummation. This passage includes—without offering a logical sequence that can be reduced to a timeline—the resurrection of Jesus from the dead (v. 20), our future resurrection with Christ (v. 23), the Second Coming of Jesus (v. 23), the end (possibly to be understood as the "end" of the end times; v. 24), the full consummation of the kingdom of God (vv. 24-25), the destruction of all (rebellious) dominion, authority and power (v. 24), the final destruction of death, the "last enemy" (v. 26; see Rev 20:13-14), and the ultimate sovereignty and glory of God as the whole of the renewed cosmos is gathered under the headship of Jesus (v. 28; see Eph 1:20-22). In the light of this we should understand death as "our last enemy."

Christians take death *more* seriously than pagans and superspiritual Corinthians, partly because it is such a violent interruption of the completeness of our bodily life. But Christians take death *less* seriously than some others because death is ultimately a conquered foe making its last desperate attack. Christ's resurrection proves that death is not an insurmountable enemy. But in the interim between Christ's resurrection and ours, death still has power (though limited) over us.

Question 7. In 1 Corinthians 6:12-14 Paul deals with the dominant Greek view of the body that persisted in the Corinthian church. The assumption behind the Corinthian heresy is that both the body and sex will be destroyed in the end, and therefore going to female prostitutes, as some Corinthian men did, was irrelevant. Paul absolutely disagrees. The body is not made for sexual immorality *but for the Lord* and, more remarkable still, "the Lord for the body" (6:13). Then Paul makes the link between our present bodily life and our future resurrection: "By his power God raised the Lord from the dead, and he will raise us also"(6:14). So the work of redemption (salvation) involves the whole person, and this includes the body. In lapsing from a biblical view of personhood the Corinthians were looking forward to a spiritual salvation in which they would be finally divested of their bodies. This agrees substantially with the Greek view that the soul and spirit were immortal but the body along with the rest of the material order would ultimately be destroyed (Fee, *First Epistle,* pp. 253-58).

In the Gospels there is a profound hint that even the soul is not immortal (Mt 10:28) and needs resurrection along with the body. Further, Paul teaches that the body is not the soul's prison, but the Spirit's temple (1 Cor 6:19). The enemy is death, not the body. And salvation is not the release of the soul from the body but the release of *both* from the transcendent power of flesh (life before Christ) by the transcendent power of the Spirit: God's end-times presence and power. Thus resurrection of the body is a new act of creation tied to God's final act of salvation and does not begin with each individual death. It is not a transition from this life to the next, as would be implied in the immortality of the soul. It comes at the end (Cullmann, *Immortality,* p. 38).

This necessarily raises the question of the state of those who have died prior to the Second Coming of Christ and the general resurrection. While the New Testament gives only sparse notice of this question, it uses various words to describe this—"with Christ," "in paradise," "under the altar" and "asleep." Even Paul appears to combine his strong belief in our personal resurrection at the return of Christ with the certainty of being in the presence of the Lord at the moment of death (2 Cor 5:6-8; Phil 1:23). On death the saints enter a deeper degree of communion with Christ, while for those not in Christ, disembodiment means entering a deeper degree of darkness. The timing of the final transformation takes us beyond calendars and clocks. F. F. Bruce wisely suggests "that in the consciousness of the departed believer there is no interval between dissolution and earth-bound human history" (H. J. Kreitzer, "The Intermediate State," in *Dictionary of Paul and His Letters,* ed. Gerald Hawthorne, Ralph Martin and Daniel Reid [Downers

Grove, Ill.: InterVarsity Press, 1993], p. 440).

Question 8. Paul's discussion of the continuity and discontinuity of our present natural body and our future spiritual body informs us of all we need to know, though less than we might wish to know. J. I. Packer says this new body will be a perfect vehicle for the Christian's self-expression, communication and relationships, including seeing and enjoying God, perfect personal integration, freedom from all frustration and evil, fulfilling all continuing desires, a sense of completeness in relation to all that is remembered as incomplete in this world, stable sinlessness, and active work and unending personal growth ("Notes on Systematic Theology IV," Regent College, Vancouver, B.C.).

For this we need to be clothed outwardly (2 Cor 5:4) as we have been inwardly made anew. The discussion takes place against the backdrop of the whole chapter that there is *one* risen Body and *one* spiritual Body, that of the Lord Jesus. Therefore our hope of an incorruptible body (Phil 3:21) is guaranteed. We are further assured of this as we are *presently* being transfigured into the likeness of Christ by the presence and power of the Holy Spirit (2 Cor 3:18).

Question 10. The first meaning of this beautiful promise relates to the Christian activities explored in verses 12-19: preaching (v. 14), believing (v. 14), truthful testimony (v. 15), faith for the present (v. 17), forgiveness for the past (v. 17) and hope for the future (vv. 18-19). But Paul holds a larger view of the implication of resurrection for personal morality and daily work in this world, as suggested in the notes on question 7.

Study 7. The Beautiful Judgment of God. Malachi 2:17—3:5; 3:13—4:3.
Purpose: To discover how the future judgment of God brings meaning to the present through repentance, faith and hope.

Questions 1 and 3. Malachi was writing in the period after the temple was rebuilt. In spite of Ezekiel's prophesies from exile in Babylon that the glory would return to the temple (Ezek 43:1-5), there was no miraculous event to mark the Lord's return to the temple and little outward encouragement to believe in God.

To those who "wearied" God with their complaint that sin seemed to be successful, Malachi prophesies of the coming of a messenger (or angel) *and* of the Lord himself to the temple. Jewish commentators interpreted the "messenger of the covenant" as Elijah; Christian interpreters have often combined the messenger and the Lord into a single personage and view this as fulfilled in the coming of Christ to cleanse the temple. While the people of Malachi's day claimed to be "seeking the Lord" (3:1), they would find the day of the Lord less comforting than they expected (see Amos 5:18). Those persisting in sin, as we shall soon see, will get their due, but even the righteous will be purified.

Question 4. The concept of covenant (God's unconditional agreement to belong to his people) is fundamental to Malachi's teaching. Because of the covenant God views himself as Israel's Father (1:6; 2:10) and wants to bless his children (3:10-12). Thus the essence of Israel's sin was a breach of relationship with God. Both priests and people failed to love God (1:6, 13; 3:8) and as a consequence promoted broken relationships in society, including divorce (2:14, 16). It is because of this fundamental covenantal relationship that God is determined in his judgment not to obliterate his people but to cleanse them. To do this the Lord must first cleanse the priesthood and then the immorality of the people. The order is significant. So are the metaphors chosen to describe the judgment of God. The refiner does not intend destruction but purification. So does the fuller's soap (really alkali), the latter being used to whiten cloth. Many of the prophets use the refiner's image, and with good reason, as J. Neil suggests: "The beauty of this picture is that the refiner looks into the open furnace, or pot, and knows that the process of purification is complete, and the dross all burnt away, when he can see his image plainly reflected in the molten metal" (*Everyday Life in the Holy Land* [Church's Ministry Among the Jews, 1913], p. 163).

Question 6. Fundamental to the biblical idea of judgment is that it is not merely a collection of individuals that will be judged but the *community* that is purified by removing the base elements. The people concerned are not merely sinners but those who will not repent. So the Lord has no alternative but to grant them their unspoken request—to live away from him in the deprivation of all that is good. Judgment is based on facts already known and choices already made. The entire Bible, and especially the New Testament, shows that human beings sentence themselves to hell in advance by loving darkness rather than light (Jn 3:19-21).

Question 7. The basis of judgment throughout the Bible, and certainly here, is our works as an evidence of true heart condition (Mt 12:36; 25:35-40; Rom 2:16; 1 Cor 4:5; 2 Cor 5:10; Rev 20:12). Except for sorcery, the sins mentioned all have a social bearing: breaking the marriage covenant, perjuring oneself (2:10-16) and so becoming untrustworthy, underpaying employees, and oppressing powerless widows and orphans (people who are the special concern of God in the covenant obligations—Ex 22:22-24; Lev 19:10). Biblical faith is never *merely* personal but always involves public discipleship and social justice. In these matters, as Joyce Baldwin says, "Malachi is the faithful pastor who faces his people with the possibility of ultimate rejection but hopes all the time to win them" (*Haggai, Zechariah, Malachi: An Introduction and Commentary* [Downers Grove, Ill.: InterVarsity Press, 1972], p. 244).

Question 9. Malachi once again takes up the theme that the "arrogant" (3:15) appear to thrive, a subject that concerned the psalmist as well (Ps 73:2-14). Those who were complaining are probably the same people as those "who feared the Lord," only they now have taken the rebuke, repented and encouraged each other to renew their faith. To demonstrate further that God's judgment is his *saving* judgment, Malachi reports the Lord's listening response (3:16) and the believers' security that they will not be forgotten in the Lord's record of names of those who are his (Ex 32:32-33; Ps 69:28; 87:6; Dan 12:1; Rev 21:27). Verses 17-18 offer the joy of covenant security and covenant consummation (you are mine and I am yours). Simultaneously, they offer a positive incentive to repent now, rather than wait for the final and irrevocable separation (v. 18). As J. I. Packer says:

> Judgment will be vindicatory, establishing justice, rather than vindictive, expressing malice. For God to judge justly is his glory, for which he is to be praised; his self-vindication is glorious (Rev 19:1-5). For God not to judge would be destructive of all serious morality and all moral responsibility. ("Notes on Systematic Theology IV")

Question 10. Malachi repeats the judgment-by-fire metaphor but now with a disturbing twist. The wicked who do not serve God (3:18) will not experience the fire as purifying but as final destruction. The same day produces gold and "tropical heat, when parched vegetation suddenly catches fire and dry fields become one vast oven in which even the roots of the plants are reduced to ash" (Baldwin, *Malachi*, p. 250). But the righteous who serve God (3:18) will experience "a fair morning of God, as when dawn comes to those who have been sick and sleepless through the night, and its beams bring healing. . . . They break into life and energy, like calves leaping from the dark pen into the sunshine" (George Adam Smith, *The Book of the Twelve Prophets, Vol. 2*, rev. ed. [New York: Harper & Row, 1928], pp. 362-63).

Study 8. Imagining the New Heaven and the New Earth. Ezekiel 43:1-12; 47:1-12.

Purpose: To show how the ultimate Christian homeland is both heaven *and earth*.

Question 1. Ezekiel's spiritual pilgrimage was a parable of the experience of the Israelites in exile. He was removed from his ministry as priest in the temple and plunged into an exilic existence. There, stripped of his old securities, he was led by God to consider in parable, allegory and vision the sin of Jerusalem and the holiness of God. Then, as a further relinquishment, Ezekiel suffered the loss of his beloved wife (24:15-24), a prophetic symbol of the speechless grief to be experienced by the exiles when their beloved Jerusalem would finally fall in 587 B.C. Now there was nothing left but God himself, the greatest treasure of all. So the last section of this book, chapters 40—48, is pure contemplation. The vision of the restored temple, the ideal Jerusalem and the renewed creation take us beyond "the things of God" to attend to God himself. The vision of heaven in the last book of the Bible has the same empowering effect on our faith.

Question 3. In chapters 40—43 Ezekiel describes his vision of a renewed temple in Jerusalem which was perfectly symmetrical and designed to exalt the holiness of God. Everything was a perfect fit in this ideal dwelling place for God. The elaborate description of the design, appointments and regulations of this temple have been interpreted by Christians in four ways: (1) as a literal prophetic blueprint of what Ezekiel intended to have rebuilt when the exiles would finally return to Jerusalem (even though some parts of the vision are logistically impossible), (2) as symbolic of the spiritual reality of the Christian church (though the vision must have meant something to the original readers), (3) as a literal future temple that, according to dispensational teaching, will be built in the last times when Israel is consummated in the kingdom age with Jesus (which again casts doubt on the relevance of this Scripture to Ezekiel's compatriots), and (4) as an accepted apocalyptic piece of literature which uses highly symbolic language to express realities that will be experienced when the story of God's people is brought to a worthy end with the coming of the Messiah (John B. Taylor, *Ezekiel: An Introduction and Commentary* [Downers Grove, Ill.: InterVarsity Press, 1969], p. 24). The heart of the vision is the exquisite promise "This is where I will live along the Israelites forever" (43:7).

Questions 4-6. "That you may know that I am the Lord" is a phrase that occurs sixty-six times in the book of Ezekiel. It captures the essence of this remarkable Old Testament book. It also locates our deepest need—to become increasingly aware of the glory of God as the ultimate reality. Like Ezekiel, who wrote and ministered in exile in faraway Babylon after 597 B.C., we live an exilic existence in this world, longing for our ultimate homeland— heaven. Ezekiel and his compatriots were surrounded by the seductions of a sophisticated but pagan foreign culture. What they needed were not mere words about God but an empowering vision that would fortify their imagination and evoke their faith. This book is not God-talk but a revelation of God, not so much in propositions but images, signs and metaphors of God's glory.

But Ezekiel has another important reason for framing his message in allegories, metaphors and parables. His message is one of judgment and hope for Jerusalem—the church of his day. He prophesied not *to* Jerusalem but *of* Jerusalem to his fellow exiles who still lived for Jerusalem and home. But Ezekiel's message about Jerusalem would be hard to speak and harder still to hear. The people who remained in Jerusalem after the first deportation, which took Ezekiel and his wife to Babylon in 597 B.C., were given to idolatrous and perverted imaginations (chap. 8). The leaders no longer led (chap. 34). The nation was like a valley of dry bones (chap. 37). To communicate the tragedy, as well as the hope of God's covenanted people, Ezekiel needed art to catch people's attention with images and stories that would draw them into a divine perspective on the matter. At times Ezekiel becomes an incarnated audiovisual aid when he lies on his side outside his house for part of each day for a year, makes models of Jerusalem with siege works and forgoes even mourning the death of his wife (24:15-27). In these things, too, Ezekiel's passion was that the people should "know that I am the Lord." For even in judging the church of that day, God will reveal himself as a faithful covenant partner.

It is this passion for the glory of God and this appeal to our redeemed imagination that gives this book its universal and timeless quality. Like Ezekiel, we are away from home, longing for our true homeland, distressed that the community that bears God's glory on earth does so in such a tawdry way and wondering what will come of it all. What we need is an empowering vision of the magnificence of God who is absolutely determined to glorify himself and to be known. The result should be repentance and a deeper hunger for God himself.

Questions 9-10. Ezekiel sees a river emerging from beneath the temple and flowing all the way to the Dead Sea, where it turns the salt water into fresh, supporting fishing in the most dead of all seas! Along the sides are trees that provide both fruit and healing. In the new heaven and the new earth proclaimed by John in the Revelation these two images are incorporated into the Holy City, the New Jerusalem. Paul Beasley-Murray notes that in Ezekiel's vision "the source of the nation's blessing in the New Age will be none other than Jehovah in his sanctuary . . . while John in the New Testament Apocalypse has characteristically used its figures to portray the spiritual blessings of the Church in the age of consummation (Rev 22:2)" (F. Davidson, ed., *The New Bible Commentary* [London: Inter-Varsity Press, 1961], p. 666).

Far from decrying the use of imagination or images, Scripture is designed to evoke our imagination. Ezekiel is so hard for us to understand precisely because we are so alienated from a full biblical spirituality. God's glory must be seen and not just talked about. Theologians today need to paint pictures and tell stories if they want people to know God. Cheryl Forbes makes this insightful summary: "Few Western theologians have considered imagination as a means to worship. Eastern Orthodoxy comes much closer to a theology of imagination, if I may so term it. The Eastern view of worship, metaphor, and image demands that imagination play a central role in interpreting Christianity" (*New Bible Commentary*, p. 24).

The orthodox theologian Berdeyev is attributed with the statement that God created the world by imagination. It is equally true to say that God will re-create the world by imagination.

Study 9. Waiting with Hope. Matthew 25:1-13, 31-46.

Purpose: To show how the Christian hope inspires a willingness to plan for a long-term future and to live constructively until the Lord comes.

Question 1. The custom of the day required that on the evening of the wedding day the bridegroom would lead the bride home, accompanied by friends and people carrying lamps in honor of the couple. The groom's exact time of arrival could never be predicted, and the crucial thing was to be ready. Sometimes the festivities lasted as long as seven days.

Both the wise and foolish were ready for a short wait; both wanted the groom to come; both had lamps with oil in them; when there was a delay, both slept. But only the wise had provided what would be needed for a long wait.

Questions 2-3. Eschatology is concerned about the Second Coming of Christ and all the realities associated with that (the resurrection of the body, the full coming of the kingdom, the last judgment and so on). Futurology can be defined as the science of how we are to live on planet earth until the end. This parable invites the exploration of how biblical eschatology relates to futurology. There are several views about how these two concepts should be combined. Some Christians hold to an eschatology with *no* futurology. They believe that Christ will come tonight, or tomorrow at the latest. So there is nothing to do in this world except prepare for the coming of the Lord. Some Christians have an eschatology with a limited futurology. They believe this is the terminal generation and we have, at best, a short time to wait. However, this results in a totally otherworldly perspective in which one abandons any will to work on the problems we face, such as the problems of ecology, or the unjust food distribution in the world. Preparing for a life of service to God as an educator, a scientist, a craftsperson or a businessperson seems secondary to the imperative of preaching God's Word and being financially supported in mission work. It is often argued that this was exactly the perspective of both Jesus and Paul, namely, that they did not believe in a future beyond their own generation. Careful biblical scholarship, however, shows that both Jesus and Paul spoke of the certainty and the character of the end of human history but said almost nothing about the timing. While they were ready for the end to come at any moment, they did not base their actions or their ethics on the certainty that the end must come soon.

While our way of life in this world must be influenced by the shortness of time, the real reason for our living in this world differently from the thoroughgoing secularist is the fact that the kingdom has come and will come fully one day. So Luther is reported to have said, "If I knew that tomorrow the world would perish, I would still plant a little apple tree in my backyard." The New Testament invites Christians to have an eschatology with a long-term futurology. They are ready for the Lord to come back at any moment, but they are also ready to work in this world in the light of that glorious certainty for another thousand years if necessary.

Question 5. Verse 31 alludes to Zechariah 14:5, a vision of the final judgment. In this case all the nations are gathered, including, it may fairly be assumed, believers, here called the "righteous." Interestingly, the sheep and goats of Palestine look very similar.

Question 6. A disturbing feature of the parable is the emphasis on determining one's eternal destiny on the basis of works. This, however, is also the criterion in Revelation 20:12-13 and the whole of the New Testament. Personal faith must inevitably be expressed by one's works. If there is no love, there is no spiritual life. The righteous enter the kingdom fully while the unrighteous depart to a place not really prepared *for them* (v. 41).

Questions 7-8. The most remarkable feature of the parable is the surprise of both the righteous and the unrighteous. The righteous were not conscious that in caring for the brothers and sisters of Christ—presumably other needy Christians—they were caring for Christ. And the unrighteous insist that if they had known they were doing it to Jesus, they would have acted compassionately. It is this factor that is hardest to understand and invites us to brood on the meaning of the parable. The person with Christ in his or her heart will help the poor because they are poor and because they are anticipating the coming kingdom, not merely because there is a reward for doing so. It is that which makes us truly kin to Jesus. The cruciality of true fellowship with Jesus is consistent with the message of the parable of the virgins in which the foolish ones were told, "I don't know you" (v. 12) by the groom.

Study 10. Speeding the End. 2 Peter 3.

Purpose: To explore what part believers play in the final unfolding of God's purposes for the world.

Question 1. It is sometimes argued that today things are so different from the world of the apostles that we are asking completely different questions about the end. But the Roman Empire was, at the time, not too different from our own society. It was in rampant decay. There was widespread homosexuality; family life was poor; marriage was despised as each man had a mistress for pleasure and a wife for domestic purposes; slavery and poverty abounded. To become a Christian meant joining a radical and despised sect, to be persecuted at any moment, to experience losing one's job or to suffer social rejection. The alternatives available today were substantially present then: *false hope,* such as that offered today by Marxism and magic, and *no hope,* as preached by existentialists and postmodern liberals. In contrast, Christian hope is immensely relevant and reassuring.

Question 3. This letter was probably written not long before Peter's martyrdom (A.D. 66-67) after he received news concerning false teachers in the church. Peter's response, intended to stimulate wholesome thinking (v. 1; see 1:12), points to the power and reliability of God's Word through which the world was created, partly destroyed in the flood and is being sustained until the right time. Not only has God kept his word, but everything has not proceeded without interruption since the beginning, as charged by the scoffers. If water was the means of destruction during the flood, fire will be the means of destruction at the end. Whether this fiery cosmic end means total annihilation or purification leading to a *transformed* cosmos is not entirely clear from the text, although the comparison made with the flood suggests the latter. God's ultimate purpose is not the destruction of what he has made but its transfiguration and ultimate glorification in the new heaven and the new earth, as Peter says (v. 13).

Question 4. The question of God's approach to time alludes to Psalm 90:4 and suggests that what we deem as delay may, from the perspective of eternity, be the very opposite: an intentioned gift of time for people to repent and for the gospel to be preached to every nation (Mk 13:10). The apostle Paul modeled a person living for the end, even hastening the coming of the Lord by proclaiming the gospel, but doing so in an *unhurried* way.

Question 5. The comparison of the Lord's coming with a thief's visit in the night is consistent with Matthew 24:43 and 1 Thessalonians 5:2. The metaphor emphasizes the need for readiness, *not* the imminence of the event, a readiness that Jesus and the apostles constantly emphasized. The superlative challenge implicit in this study is to be ready even if the event is not necessarily imminent.

Question 6. Peter uses apocalyptic language reminiscent of Mark 13:24 and Isaiah 34:4. But to say that the language is figurative is not to say it is unrelated to reality. As we have repeatedly seen, the Second Coming of Christ is associated with the end of the world *as we now know it* and the introduction, through a means that transcends our reasoning, of a new heaven *and a new earth*. That there is a correspondence between this world and the next is powerfully stated. That there is a radical discontinuity between the two worlds is the point Peter is making. This world will not simply make a pleasant transition into utopia through human effort with a little divine assistance. There will be a transformation, and that transformation is associated with the greatest event of all—the Second Coming of Jesus.

Questions 7-9. Peter's intention is neither to inspire feverish dread nor idle preparedness. By envisioning the Lord's coming and by anticipating the new heaven and the new earth, which is the "home of righteousness" (v. 13), Peter invites his readers (and us) to prepare themselves to go home. His motivation to holy living and living in peace with God (v. 14) is not simply founded on the possible nightmare of being caught unprepared, an appeal that has its focus more on fear than faith. Rather, Peter invites us to envision the new heaven and the new earth, the age of grace, the patience of God, and the opportunity of embracing the coming of the Lord *now* through appropriate living. These appeal to true faith. So today, not tomorrow, is the day to repent and to begin working out one's own salvation. We are surrounded and upheld in this by the grace of God (v. 18). Indeed, it is only as we keep growing in that grace that the possibility of falling can be avoided (v. 17; 1 Pet 2:1-2).

In his commentary on 2 Peter, Michael Green notes that waiting for the Lord Jesus does not mean pious inactivity:

> It means action. . . . It is intended to be a time of cooperation with God in the redemption of society. Our era between the advents is the age of grace, the age of the Spirit, the age of evangelism. But while evangelism would seem to be the main way in which we can be said to hasten the coming of the Lord (cf. Mk. xiii.10), we cannot confine our preparations to evangelism. We cannot exclude the prayer, "Thy kingdom come" (cf. Rev. viii.4); nor Christian behaviour (verse 11, and see 1 Pet. ii.12); nor repentance and obedience (Acts iii.19-21). All these contribute to the ultimate goal. . . . It is Christian listlessness, disobedi-

ence and lovelessness which delay *the coming of the day of God.* (Michael Green, *The Second Epistle of Peter and the Epistle of Jude* [Grand Rapids, Mich.: Eerdmans, 1979], p. 140)

Question 52 of the Heidelberg Catechism addresses the way the gospel inspires personal confidence as we anticipate the coming of Christ: "What comfort has thou by the coming of Christ to judge the quick and the dead?" Answer: "That in all my miseries and persecutions I look with my head erect for the very same, who before yielded Himself unto the judgment of God for me and took away all malediction from me, to come as Judge from heaven."

Study 11. Making Forever Friends. Luke 16.

Purpose: To discover how to use one's money in light of the end.

Questions 1-3. The two parables in this chapter are found only in Luke. Each detail of a parable, while significant to the ending, is not given as an example to be followed. Sometimes Jesus uses dishonest characters to make his point, as in the parable of the shrewd manager. Far from encouraging deceit, Jesus, in a triple level of meaning, first makes the manager commend the dishonest steward for shrewdness (v. 8), then comments on the financial shrewdness of people outside the people of God, and finally calls for a special kind of financial shrewdness among the children of light.

Question 4. Jesus' attitude toward money in this section is complex. On the one hand, it is "unrighteous" or "worldly" and therefore tainted. He apparently would not agree with those who claim that wealth or riches is a problem only through the way it is used. While the Bible does *not* say that money itself is a root of all evil (only the *love* of money—1 Tim 6:10), Jesus warns against the propensity of wealth to become an alternative center of life (v. 13). Apparently it was such to the Pharisees (v. 14), who regarded their wealth as a reward for their careful observance of the law, thus bringing a deeper irony to the encounter. The ambiguity of money does not mean, however, that the Christian should eliminate the problem by adopting voluntary poverty. Just the reverse, as we shall see. In this extraordinary parable and the challenging commentary on it, Jesus invites the redemption of mammon by outdoing the pagan in shrewdness: using it to make friends that will last even in the next life. Handling money in this life is an important preparation for the next (v. 11). The next parable shows how *not* to do this, and by offering a negative example, invites an imaginative positive response.

Question 5. As a master storyteller Jesus uses an economy of words to create a vivid picture. Not immediately apparent is that the name Lazarus means "God is my helper," a fact that would be obvious to Jesus' first hearers and may partly explain why, without any other reason being given, he ended up in Jewish heaven: the bosom of Abraham. But in this life the beggar was largely ignored by the rich man who apparently regarded the beggar as a "fixture" in the estate.

It takes little imagination to consider how the relationship of these two might have been different. The theological reason behind the needed change, however, is not so obvious. Biblically we do not own anything absolutely, but have a trust from God. So John Chrysostom, the fourth-century preacher, was substantially right when he said that the rich hold their goods as stewards for the poor. In a global village this becomes even more challenging.

Question 6. In contrast to a strategy widely used in Christian apologetics— proving the historical resurrection of Jesus as a foundation for faith—Jesus considers that his own (coming) resurrection will have no effect on those people who are not obeying the Word they already have from God. The example from the law chosen by Jesus is divorce, alongside his general reference to the Law and Prophets, which call for mercy and justice. It is seldom mentioned that failure to be willing to live according to the obligations of God's covenant predisposes one *not* to believe at all.

Questions 7-10. The thrust of Luke 16 is the call to use our money to make friends with the poor, the sick, the powerless, the stranger and the refugee. These two parables make the daring claim that what we gain through befriending the poor is love. Often the poor are richer than the rich in the treasures that really matter: relationships.

In a series of sermons on the rich man and Lazarus, John Chrysostom argues for a stewardship approach to money. Appealing to the prophets of the Old Testament (Mal 3:8-10), Chrysostom warns about the spiritual dangers of the rich. Failing to share with the poor will be counted as theft. The rich "hold the goods of the poor even if they have inherited them from their fathers or no matter how they gathered their wealth." "The most pitiable person of all," he says, "is the one who lives in luxury and shares his goods with nobody." In contrast, *"By nourishing Christ* in poverty here and laying up great profit hereafter we will be able to attain the good things which are to come" (*On Wealth and Poverty,* trans. Catherine P. Roth [Crestwood, N.Y.: St. Vladimir's Seminary Press, 1984], pp. 49, 57, 55, emphasis mine). In this last quotation Chrysostom hints that ministering to the poor simultaneously heals the hearts of the rich and nourishes Jesus himself.

Study 12. Investing in Heaven. 1 Thessalonians 4:13—5:11; 2 Thessalonians 3:6-18.
Purpose: To discover the connection between work in this world and the Second Coming of Jesus.
Questions 1-3. To reassure those whose loved ones died before the Lord's return, Paul explains how there will be no disadvantage to those who have died—they will be resurrected to meet Jesus. But those who remain will be caught up to meet Jesus. The word used here has given rise to a doctrine called "the rapture": the evacuation of believers from the earth prior to the time of the great tribulation. While people have differing views about whether the text will allow us to say this much, it is important not to lose the beauty and meaning of Paul's words. Just as the leading citizens in a Greek city would go out to meet a visiting dignitary, escorting him on the final stage of the journey, so the Lord is pictured as escorted to the earth by his people, both those newly resurrected and those who were alive at his coming. The heart of it is simply that we will be with Jesus and he will be with us. Not even death can separate us from the glory of that reunion.
Questions 6-7. In the Greek world work was a curse. For Paul it was a ministry. But the Thessalonians would have been deeply influenced by the Greek view that unemployment allowed one to participate in the political domain and to enjoy the contemplative life. An individual's activity in society was called *ergon* or *ponos,* a burden and toil. During the fifth century before Christ, the government of Thebes issued a decree prohibiting its citizens from engaging in work! But there was a further problem in Thessalonica: eschatological idleness. If Jesus might come back tomorrow, what is the point of working today? Missing the opportunity to work by faith, love and hope (1 Thess 1:3), believers wanted to "see" the results of their work or they would not work at all. Let others look after them as they move from house to house absorbing Christian hospitality like sponges. Hence Paul's blunt word (2 Thess 3:10).
Question 8. Workaholics try to find their identity and fulfillment in their work, whether it is mothering, administering or preaching. Usually raised in nonaffirming environments, workaholics are attempting, often unconsciously, to prove themselves worthy of the approval of their parents. Workaholics are consumed by this inner drivenness and cannot play without feeling guilty. Workaholics have to work at play and cannot play at work. It is too serious a matter because, lacking a sense of their own creatureliness, they make an idol out of their work. Idolatry, simply defined, is making something one's ultimate concern other than the One who is ultimate. Amos may be describing workaholics when he rails against the people who spend their sabbaths figuring out

how to make more money as soon as it is over (Amos 8:5). The whole of life is oriented around what becomes one continuous work week. Workaholics easily "use" people to climb the ladder of success and easily manipulate others, often under the guise of "caring" and "helping." But the outside effect of the workaholic is the same as the idler (the subject of Paul's concern).

Workaholics are a burden to those around them, requiring people to constantly adjust their lives and priorities to the all-consuming nature of the workplace. And workaholics have nothing to give to those they live with except money—no affection, no joy, no friendship, no companionship, no love. They are emotional and relational thieves in the family and the community. On the outside they are burdens and have nothing to give. But the inside comparison fares no better.

Both the idler and the workaholic show symptoms of moral sloth. Neither has gone deep enough to see that the reason to work as Christians is not simply for personal expression and to meet personal needs. *Work is a divine vocation,* a calling. As a vocation it is not something we take on ourselves or choose as a way of fulfilling ourselves. Rather, it is something we do in response to a divine summons. So it is God we are pleasing in our work, and it turns out that God is often easier to please than our parents! According to Luther, virtually all occupations are modes of "full-time" service to God except those of the usurer, the prostitute and the monk. A biblical theology of calling embraces more than simply fulfilling one's obligations in one or more sectors of our life situation: congregation, family, neighbor, state and the cosmos. Rather, work is our total service to God in all these spheres for the purposes of the kingdom. In this larger sense we cannot speak of "choosing one's vocation" because we have been chosen and called (Eph 4:1)! Rather we speak of living for God in the totality of our lives and discovering God's grace in the concrete realities of the work world, especially in light of the end.

Study 13. Going to the Lamb's Wedding. Revelation 7:9-17; 19:1-10; 21:1-9.
Purpose: To show how our relationship to Christ as his people should be shaped by the vision of our final home with God.
Question 1. Our opening study takes us to heaven, where the great international gathering of saints assembles before the throne of God and the Lamb (see also 4:1-2; 5:6). The Revelation of John ushers us into a world of dragons, beasts, angels, cosmic catastrophes and martyrs chanting hymns. We are swept from one riveting vision to the next as we are transported from heaven to earth and back again, in an upstairs-downstairs drama. Bowls of judgment

are poured out on the earth while cringing multitudes call on the hills to cover them from the wrath of the Lamb. There is a final battle, a wonderful wedding supper and an exquisite garden city. In this book we are overwhelmed with visions of complex creatures, stylized presentations of Jesus that defy literal interpretation (Rev 1:12-18) and ghastly, though victorious, battles against a demonized culture and world system.

Partly because of the unusual nature of apocalypse, modern Christians, unable to appreciate its symbolic quality, sometimes reduce the images of the book to a series of timeline events that are made to correspond with contemporary newscasts. It is not surprising that there are many opinions surrounding the Revelation, especially concerning the enigmatic phrase in 20:6 concerning the so-called millennial reign. J. I. Packer says, "Opinions vary as to (i) what the world will look like when Christ reappears (postmillennialism says Christianized; pre- and a-millennialism says apostate); (ii) whether the church will be raptured from the earth prior to judgment day (premillennialism says yes, others say no); (iii) whether Christ will appear on earth prior to the judgment day (premillennialists say yes, others say no); (iv) whether, under the earthly reign of Christ that premillennialism posits, God will fulfil special purposes for the Jewish people, outside and apart from the Christian Church" ("Notes on Systematic Theology IV"). The constellation of realities surrounding the appearance of Christ include the personal appearing of Jesus in glory, the resurrection of the dead, final judgment and cosmic renewal. The certainty of this nourishes a deep hope. But the exact order and many of the details remain a mystery.

Questions 3-4. John's pastoral interest is especially apparent in his choice of the central metaphor of the spiritual life in the Revelation: the martyr. After the introductory letters to the churches in Asia (Rev 1—3), we do not meet in John's twenty-two chapters a single living Christian left on earth. All the Christians one meets in vision after vision are martyrs. The Greek word "witness" (*martyr*) is invested with its second meaning: the Christian is simply one who loses his life in order to find another life in Jesus. It is irrelevant whether one does this stage by stage or in one extravagant act. The challenge of living this metaphor is simply this: either overcome with Jesus, or be overcome by the red dragon, beast, harlot and Babylon. Overcomers are not supersaints but mere Christians.

A Celtic text—an Irish homily of the seventh century—takes up the idea that martyrdom was the normal spiritual outlook of the early Christians and expresses some of the options in a society less hostile though more seductive: Red martyrdom consists of death for Jesus' sake. Green martyrdom consists of fasting and labor through which the believer flees from his evil desires and lives a life of repentance. White martyrdom consists of abandoning everything one loves for the sake of God (Timothy Ware, *The Orthodox Church* [Harmondsworth, England: Penguin, 1983], p. 23). Eugene Peterson shows that by cultivating the praying imagination, John helps us *see* enough to live the martyr metaphor whether red, green or white: "The contribution of the Revelation to the work of witness is not instruction, telling us how to make a coherent apology of the faith, but imagination, strengthening the spirit with images that keep us 'steadfast, immovable, always abounding in the work of the Lord' (1 Cor 15:58). Instruction in witness is important, but courage is critical, for it takes place in the pitched battle" (Eugene H. Peterson, *Reversed Thunder: The Revelation and the Praying Imagination* [San Francisco: Harper & Row, 1988], p. 112).

Question 5. In this chapter and in the last two chapters, when Christ makes all things new, John envisions an endless environment of worship in which the greatest gift is seeing God's face (22:4). John's business as a pastor is to keep his people dealing with God, and worship does this better than anything. Indeed, in this book everyone worships. Unless we worship God we will inevitably worship the evil trinity: the beast, the harlot and the false prophet, joining those who choose to be sent to hell singing pseudo-hymns: "Who is like the beast?" According to John, it is impossible not to worship.

Question 6. John accomplishes his purpose of empowering the saints to live triumphantly by pulling back the curtain of "normal" perception to let us see a transcendent reality. The Lamb has triumphed even though the harlot appears to reign supreme. Heaven, for John, is not up there, or later, but bursting into the here and now. The Revelation is much more than a book of predictions. Rather than tell us what will take place, it gets right inside history to see what H. H. Rowley described as a "unique divine initiative at the end of history . . . when God would act in a way as solely His own as His act of creation had been" (H. H. Rowley, *The Relevance of Apocalyptic: A Study of Jewish and Christian Apocalypses from Daniel to the Revelation* [Greenwood, S.C.: Attic Press, 1980], p. 170). The world, according to John the apocalyptist, is both more tragic and more hopeful than is immediately apparent.

Questions 7-8. Revelation is to the Second Coming of Jesus what the Ignatian exercises are to the first coming of Jesus: they involve an imaginative presentation of the spiritual meaning of the coming of Jesus in a way designed to evoke a deep and personal encounter with the Lord himself. This cannot be done without imagination. So John envisions the consummation of the spiritual life and human history as a marriage (19:7-9; 21:2), a marriage so glorious that all direct experiences of God in this life are mere betrothal exchanges and assurances (2 Cor 11:2). This metaphor gathers up one of the great themes of the Bible: the covenant. The formula for the covenant, frequently reaffirmed in the Bible—"you are my people and I am your God"—finds its fulfillment in the final consummation: "the dwelling of God is with men, and he will live with them. They will be his people, and God himself will be with them and be their God" (Rev 21:3). The basis of this hope is the saving work of Christ, exemplified in the Lamb slain (Rev 5:6; Is 53:7; Jn 1:29). So our confidence in being invited to the wedding is not simply "righteous acts" (19:8) but acts that give evidence of one's heart condition as found in Christ by grace rather than works.

Questions 9-10. Here we take up an Old Testament prophecy about the new heaven and the new earth (Is 65:17-25). A previous study (1 Cor 15) shows that the Christian hope is not the immortality of the soul but the resurrection of the body. Now at the end of the Bible (and the end of the end times) we discover a thoroughly material environment: a garden city, music, art, movement and community. Above all else and in the center of everything is the Lamb who replaces the temple (21:22) and illuminates everything (22:5). The ultimate dignity of the people of God is to be the "bride, the wife of the Lamb" (21:9).

Question 11. In Revelation we are invited to live with an open heaven. If we "see" heaven, we will see earth the way it really is. Kingdom-consciousness is another way of speaking of this: living hopefully within the tension of the "here" and "not-yet-but-coming" kingdom of Jesus. This heavenly-mindedness is conspicuously lacking in Western Christianity today. Kingdom-consciousness delivers us from false messianism (that our work, social action, ministry and compassionate ministry will save society) and from false pessimism (that our work in this world has to be successful and "religious" to be meaningful). Like all contemplatives, apocalyptic Christians will seem a little bit irrelevant to the worldlings around.

R. Paul Stevens is the David J. Brown Professor of Marketplace Theology and Leadership at Regent College in Vancouver, British Columbia. He is also the author of the LifeGuide® Bible Studies 1 Corinthians *(coauthored with Dan Williams),* 2 Corinthians, Job *and* Revelation. *He is currently writing the LifeGuide® Bible Study* Spiritual Gifts.